DC ENTERTAINMENT™

May 2013

For decades DC Entertainment has been at the forefront of the graphic novel revolution, publishing the most acclaimed stories from the greatest talents in the industry. From Alan Moore and Dave Gibbons's WATCHMEN to Geoff Johns and Gary Frank's BATMAN: EARTH ONE, DC Comics, Vertigo and MAD have been reinforcing the graphic novel as not just a medium to entertain and excite, but also as one of popular culture's greatest art forms.

There's just one problem: Where to begin?

Right here. With the DCE ESSENTIAL GRAPHIC NOVELS AND CHRONOLOGY 2013 catalog, we're presenting an easy entry point for all those who want to know exactly how to break into our rich backlist of titles.

For new readers, this catalog will be the perfect gateway from which to start exploring the breadth and depth of DC Entertainment's comprehensive library, from the earliest DC Comics superhero tales, to cutting edge stories from Vertigo, to the irreverent humor of MAD. We realize how daunting it can be to look at a wall of graphic novels, but we hope to help guide readers to what we feel are the best entry points into not only our three imprints, but the comic book medium at large. For our dedicated fan base, this will be a refreshing look back at how our incredible talent has created the richest and most multilayered mythology in the world of comics. Hopefully this catalog will be able to expand even the most enthusiastic fan's graphic novel collection, with our spotlight titles and suggested reading chronology.

Welcome to DC Entertainment.

Jim Lee   Dan DiDio

Co-Publisher   Co-Publisher

A Warner Bros Entertainment Company

4000 Warner Blvd Burbank CA 91522

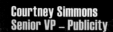

TABLE OF CONTENTS

25 ESSENTIAL

GRAPHIC NOVELS

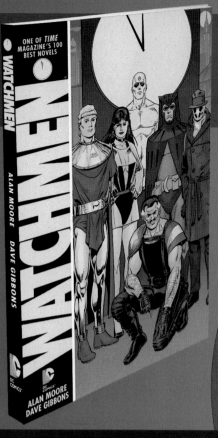

WATCHMEN
THE GREATEST GRAPHIC NOVEL OF ALL TIME

"A work of ruthless psychologica[l] realism, it's a landmark in the graphic nove[l] medium. It would be A MASTERPIECE i[n] any." —*TIME Magazine, TIME Magazine's 10*[?] best English–language novels since 1923

"REMARKABLE. The would-be heroes of WATCHME[N] have staggeringly complex psychological profiles." —*The New York Times Book Revie*[w]

"Dark, violent and blackly funny, WATCHMEN is [a] comic book like no other…. [It is] the CRIME AN[D] PUNISHMENT of graphic novels." —*London Times*

One of the most influential graphic novels of all time and a perennial bestseller, WATCHMEN is considered a gateway title to the entire graphic storytelling medium. Alan Moore and Dave Gibbons's seminal story is the benchmark against which all other graphic novels and comic books are judged.

A murder mystery-turned-nationwide conspiracy, WATCHMEN examines the lives of the eponymous superhero team as they seem to decay alongside the ever-darkening America around them. Rorschach, Nite Owl, the Silk Spectre, Dr. Manhattan and Ozymandias reunite to investigate who's behind a team-mate's murder, but find that the truth may be even more grim than the world they seek to protect.

WATCHMEN

American Edition: Writer: Alan Moore | Artist: Dave Gibbons | ISBN: 978-0-9302-8923-2 | Diamond Code: FEB058406 | Price: $19.99 | Format: TP

International Edition: Writer: Alan Moore | Artist: Dave Gibbons | ISBN: 978-1-4012-2266-6 | Diamond Code: JUL088045 | Price: $19.99 | Format: TP

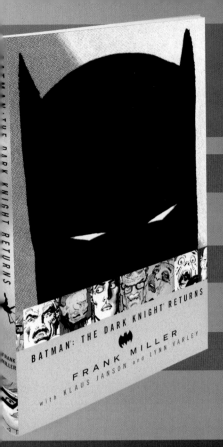

BATMAN:
THE DARK KNIGHT RETURNS
THE GREATEST BATMAN STORY EVER TOLD

"GROUNDBREAKING." —*USA Today*

"Changed the course of comics." —*Rolling Stone*

"REVISIONIST pop epic." —*SPIN*

Ten years after an aging Batman has retired, Gotham City has sunk deeper into decadence and law-lessness. Now, when his city needs him most, the Dark Knight returns in a blaze of glory. Joined by Carrie Kelly, a teenage female Robin, Batman must take back the streets.

Hailed as a comics masterpiece, THE DARK KNIGHT RETURNS is Frank Miller's (*300* and *Sin City*) reinvention of Gotham's legendary protector. It remains one of the most influential stories ever told in comics, and is a book cited by the filmmakers as an inspiration for the recent blockbuster Batman movies.

BATMAN: THE DARK KNIGHT RETURNS

Writer: Frank Miller | Artist: Frank Miller | ISBN: 978-1-5638-9342-1 | Diamond Code: NOV118095 | Price: $14.99 | Format: TP

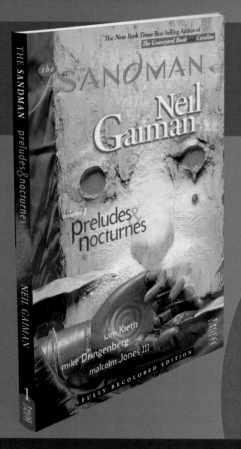

THE SANDMAN
VOL.1: PRELUDES & NOCTURNES
THE FIRST VOLUME OF THE DEFINITIVE VERTIGO SERIES BY THE LEGENDARY NEIL GAIMAN

"THE SANDMAN just might be the SMARTEST COMIC BOOK EVER WRITTEN." —*USA Today*

"Neil Gaiman's long-running series made cool comics fantastical and fantastical comics cool. THE SANDMAN is a modern myth, as well as a précis on why the stories we tell matter so much."—*Playboy*

"The greatest epic in the history of comic books."
—*Los Angeles Times Magazine*

An occultist attempting to capture Death to bargain for eternal life traps Death's younger brother Dream instead. After his seventy-year imprisonment and eventual escape, Dream, also known as Morpheus, goes on a quest for his lost objects of power to reclaim his role as the keeper of dreams.

The *New York Times* best-selling author Neil Gaiman's transcendent series THE SANDMAN is often labeled as not only the definitive Vertigo title, but also as one of the finest achievements in graphic storytelling. Gaiman created an unforgettable tale of the forces that exist beyond life and death by weaving ancient mythology, folklore and fairy tales with his own distinct narrative vision.

THE SANDMAN VOL. 1: PRELUDES & NOCTURNES

Writer: Neil Gaiman | Artists: Sam Kieth, Malcolm Jones III, Mike Dringenberg | ISBN: 978-1-5638-9011-6 | Diamond Code: JUL100259 | Price: $19.99 | Format: TP

FRANK MILLER • DAVID MAZZUCCHELLI
WITH RICHMOND LEWIS

BATMAN

YEAR ONE

BATMAN:
YEAR ONE
THE TIMELESS ORIGIN STORY OF
THE CAPED CRUSADER

"It's not only ONE OF THE MOST IMPORTANT COMICS EVER WRITTEN, it's also among the best." —IGN

"This is a story no true Batman fan should be able to resist." —*School Library Journal*

"There's never been storytelling quite like this. It took someone who views comics as an art to create it." —*Washington Post*

In 1986, Frank Miller and David Mazzucchelli produced this groundbreaking reinterpretation of the origin of Batman—who he is, and how he came to be. Sometimes careless and naive, this Dark Knight is far from the flawless vigilante he is today. In his first year on the job, Batman feels his way in a Gotham City far darker than when he left it. His solemn vow to extinguish the town's criminal element is only half the battle; along with Lieutenant James Gordon, the Dark Knight must also fight a police force more corrupt than the scum in the streets.

BATMAN: YEAR ONE is one of the greatest Batman graphic novels of all time. Timeless in its appeal, this masterpiece would stand apart from the crowded comics field even today.

BATMAN: YEAR ONE

Writer: Frank Miller | Artist: David Mazzucchelli | ISBN: 978-1-4012-0752-6 | Diamond Code: OCT060163 | Price: $14.99 | Format: TP

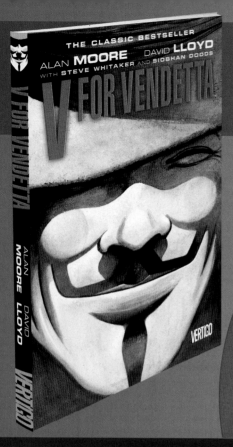

V FOR VENDETTA

A DARK PORTRAIT OF OPPRESSION AND RESISTANCE SET AGAINST THE BACKDROP OF DYSTOPIAN FUTURE ENGLAND

"DARK, GRIPPING storytelling."
—*Entertainment Weekly*

"V FOR VENDETTA has serious and resounding implications for our time and place."
—*USA Today*

"Densely packed, thematically VIBRANT and PHILOSOPHICALLY CHALLENGING."
—Scripps Howard News Service

A visionary graphic novel that defines sophisticated storytelling, Alan Moore's best-selling V FOR VENDETTA is a terrifying portrait of totalitarianism and resistance, superbly illustrated by artist David Lloyd.

Set in a futurist totalitarian England, a country without freedom or faith, a mysterious man in a white porcelain mask strikes back against the oppressive overlords on behalf of the voiceless. This powerful story detailing the loss and fight for individuality has become a cultural touchstone and an enduring allegory for current events.

V FOR VENDETTA

Writer: Alan Moore | Artist: David Lloyd | ISBN: 978-1-4012-0841-7 | Diamond Code: SEP088030 | Price: $19.99 | Format: TP

FROM THE AWARD-WINNING
WRITER OF WATCHMEN

SAGA OF THE SWAMP THING BOOK ONE

THE GROUNDBREAKING TITLE THAT LAUNCHED ALAN MOORE INTO COMICS SUPER-STARDOM

"Hyper INTELLIGENT, emotionally POTENT, and yes, FUN. A." —*Entertainment Weekly*

"Another of the true classics of the genre." —IGN

"A cerebral meditation on the state of the American soul." —NPR

Before tackling *Watchmen*, Alan Moore made his debut in the U.S. comic book industry with the revitalization of the horror comic book SWAMP THING. His deconstruction of the classic monster stretched the creative boundaries of the medium and became one of the most spectacular series in industry history.

SAGA OF THE SWAMP THING came to explore modern-day issues against a backdrop of the macabre. With a host of some of the genre's greatest artists, Alan Moore's first masterpiece for DC/Vertigo serves as a stunning commentary on environmental, political and social issues, unflinching in its relevance.

SAGA OF THE SWAMP THING BOOK ONE

Writer: Alan Moore | Artist: Stephen Bissette | ISBN: 978-1-4012-2083-9 | Diamond Code: JAN120343 | Price: $19.99 | Format: TP

11

FOR MATURE READERS

FABLES VOL. 1:
LEGENDS IN EXILE
FOLKLORE COMES TO LIFE AS THESE REAL-LIFE FAIRY TALE CHARACTERS ARE EXILED IN MODERN-DAY NEW YORK

"[A] WONDERFULLY TWISTED concept." —*Washington Post*

"An epic, beautifully written story." —*The Onion*

"GREAT FUN." —*Booklist*

The #1 *New York Times* best-selling series and winner of 14 Eisner Awards

When a savage creature known only as the Adversary conquered the homeland of legends and myth, all of the infamous inhabitants of folklore were forced into exile. Disguised among the normal citizens of modern-day New York, these magical characters created their own secret society called Fabletown. But when Snow White's party-girl sister, Rose Red, is apparently murdered, it's up to Bigby, the reformed Big Bad Wolf and Fabletown's sheriff, to find the killer.

FABLES VOL. 1: LEGENDS IN EXILE

Writer: Bill Willingham | Artists: Lan Medina & others | ISBN: 978-1-4012-3755-4 | Diamond Code: FEB120285 | Price: $12.99 | Format: TP

BATMAN:
THE KILLING JOKE
THE DELUXE EDITION
ALAN MOORE'S UNFORGETTABLE MEDITATION ON THE RAZOR-THIN LINE BETWEEN SANITY AND INSANITY, HEROISM AND VILLAINY, COMEDY AND TRAGEDY

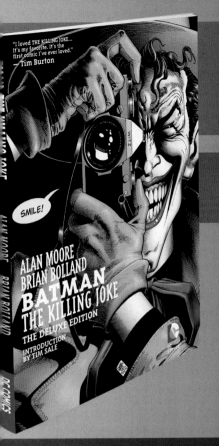

"I loved BATMAN: THE KILLING JOKE. It's my favorite. It's the first comic I ever loved."
—Tim Burton

"A GENUINELY CHILLING portrayal of Batman's greatest foe." —*Booklist*

"Easily the GREATEST JOKER STORY ever told, BATMAN: THE KILLING JOKE is also one of Alan Moore's finest works. If you've read it before, go back and read it again. You owe it to yourself." —IGN

In this groundbreaking work, Moore weaves together a twisted tale of insanity and human perseverance featuring Batman's greatest foe, the Joker.

Looking to prove that any man can be pushed past his breaking point into madness, The Joker attempts to drive Commissioner Gordon insane. Refusing to give up even after suffering a tremendous personal tragedy, Gordon struggles to maintain his sanity with the help of Batman in a desperate effort to best the madman.

BATMAN: THE KILLING JOKE: THE DELUXE EDITION

Writer: Alan Moore | Artist: Brian Bolland | ISBN: 978-1-4012-1667-2 | Diamond Code: NOV070226 | Price: $17.99 | Format: TP

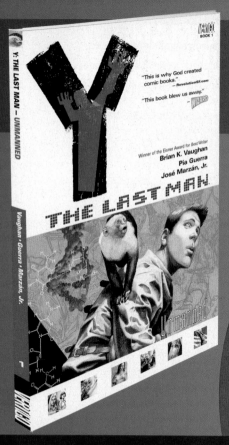

Y: THE LAST MAN
VOL. 1: UNMANNED
WHAT WOULD YOU DO IF YOU WERE THE LAST MAN ON EARTH?

"FUNNY and SCARY. An unbelievable critique of society. A+."
—*Washington Post*

"THE BEST GRAPHIC NOVEL I'VE EVER READ." —Stephen King

"This year's best movie is a comic book."
—"All Things Considered," NPR

Y: THE LAST MAN is that rare example of a page-turner that is all at once humorous, socially relevant and endlessly surprising.

Written by Brian K. Vaughan (*Lost*, *Pride of Baghdad*, *Ex Machina*) and with art by Pia Guerra, this is the saga of Yorick Brown, the only human of a planet-wide plague that instantly kills every mammal possessing a Y chromosome. Accompanied by a mysterious government agent, a brilliant young geneticist and his pet monkey, Ampersand, Yorick travels the world in search of his lost love and the answer to why he's the last man on Earth.

Y: THE LAST MAN VOL. 1: UNMANNED

Writer: Brian K. Vaughan | Artist: Pia Guerra | ISBN: 978-1-5638-9980-5 | Diamond Code: DEC108152 | Price: $14.99 | Format: TP

ALL-STAR SUPERMAN

THE CRITICALLY ACCLAIMED, GENRE-BENDING SERIES THAT HARKENS BACK TO THE GOLDEN AGE OF SUPERMAN

"A STIRRINGLY MYTHIC, EMOTIONALLY RESONANT, and gloriously alternative take on the Man of Steel." —*Entertainment Weekly*

"Maniacally brilliant."
—*The New York Times*

"Taking the Man of Steel back to his roots and into the future at the same time, ALL-STAR SUPERMAN is EXCITING, BOLD and SUPERCOOL … all the makings of a classic." —*Variety*

The Underverse ruled by Bizarros. The time-eating Chronovore. Jimmy Olsen, superhero?

Nothing is impossible in ALL-STAR SUPERMAN.

The unstoppable creative team of writer Grant Morrison and artist Frank Quitely (*We3*, *Flex Mentallo*, *JLA: Earth 2*, *New X-Men*) join forces once more to take Superman back to basics. In an emotionally and visually stunning graphic novel harkening back to a Golden Age of comics, ALL-STAR SUPERMAN creates a new, and at the same time familiar, take on the World's First Superhero.

ALL-STAR SUPERMAN

Writer: Grant Morrison | Artist: Frank Quitely | ISBN: 978-1-4012-3205-4 | Diamond Code: JUL110247 | Price: $29.99 | Format: TP

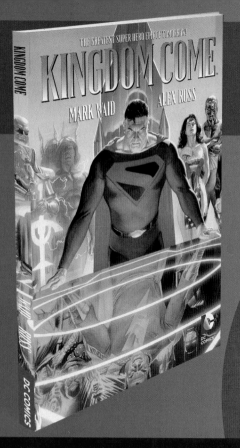

KINGDOM COME

OLD AND NEW ERAS OF SUPERHEROES ARE PITTED AGAINST EACH OTHER IN THIS EPIC GRAPHIC NOVEL

"No library should be without some edition of this book." —*Library Journal*

"Waid's charged dialogue and Ross's stunning visual realism expose the GENIUS, pride, fears and foibles of DC's heroes and villains."

—*Washington Post*

"Wagnerian. Credit Mark Waid's script for keeping the mood dark and morally muddled, but it's Alex Ross's thousand-plus watercolor panels (reproduced in captivating detail) that propel these scenes of Revelation-style apocalypse and reborn hope."

—*Village Voice*

Winner of five Eisner and Harvey Awards, KINGDOM COME is the best-selling graphic novel from acclaimed writer Mark Waid and superstar painter Alex Ross.

Set in the not-so-distant future, the DC Universe is spinning inexorably out of control. The new generation of heroes has lost their moral compass, becoming just as reckless and violent as the villains they fight. The previous regime of heroes—the Justice League—returns under the most dire of circumstances, setting up a battle of the old guard against these uncompromising protectors in a battle that will define what heroism truly is.

KINGDOM COME

Writer: Mark Waid | Artist: Alex Ross | ISBN: 978-1-4012-2034-1 | Diamond Code: JUN080246 | Price: $17.99 | Format: TP

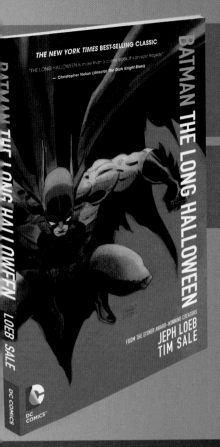

BATMAN:
THE LONG HALLOWEEN
A CLASSIC BATMAN MURDER MYSTERY BY THE ICONIC CREATIVE TEAM OF JEPH LOEB AND TIM SALE

"Stretches beyond the normal boundaries of comics to create a LEGENDARY story of one man's crusade against an insane world."—IGN

"Featuring Sale's breathtaking art, which perfectly echoes the moodiness of the subject matter, THE LONG HALLOWEEN [is] AN INSTANT CLASSIC."
—*Metro Toronto*

"More than a comic book. It's AN EPIC TRAGEDY."
—Christopher Nolan (director of *Batman Begins*, *The Dark Knight* and *The Dark Knight Rises*)

Set just after Batman's first year in Gotham City, the Dark Knight finds himself working alongside District Attorney Harvey Dent and Lieutenant James Gordon, trying to vanquish the criminal element. However, a serial killer known only as Holiday has been killing friend and foe each month. Batman races against the calendar trying to discover the assassin's identity, fighting the entirety of Gotham's rogues' gallery along the way.

The magnificent creative team of Jeph Loeb and Tim Sale reach their apex in BATMAN: THE LONG HALLOWEEN, propelling this graphic novel to its place amongst comics' finest murder mystery stories.

BATMAN: THE LONG HALLOWEEN

Writer: Jeph Loeb | Artist: Tim Sale | ISBN: 978-1-4012-3259-7 | Diamond Code: JUL110251 | Price: $24.99 | Format: TP

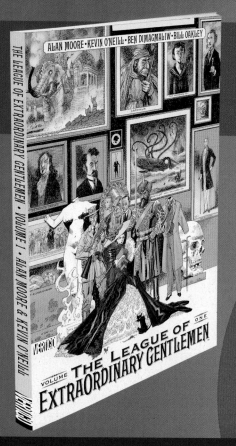

THE LEAGUE OF EXTRAORDINARY GENTLEMEN VOL. 1

PROMINENT FIGURES FROM NINETEENTH-CENTURY LITERATURE BAND TOGETHER IN ALAN MOORE'S AWARD-WINNING GRAPHIC NOVEL

"A great graphic novel. Indeed, EXTRAORDINARY." —*TIME*

"Moore has combined his love of nineteenth century literature with an IMAGINATIVE MASTERY of its twentieth century corollary, the superhero comic book." —*Publishers Weekly*

"INVENTIVE and SUSPENSEFUL."
—*Library Journal*

London, 1898. The Victorian Era draws to a close and the twentieth century approaches. It is a time of great change and stagnation, a period of chaste order and ignoble chaos. It is an era in need of champions. A League.

In this amazingly imaginative graphic novel from Alan Moore and Kevin O'Neill, the most popular turn-of-the-century literary figures are brought together to face any and all threats coming to Britain. Allan Quartermain, Mina Murray, Dr. Henry Jekyll and Edward Hyde, Captain Nemo and Hawley Griffin, the Invisible Man, form The League of Extraordinary Gentlemen.

THE LEAGUE OF EXTRAORDINARY GENTLEMEN VOL. 1

Writer: Alan Moore | Artist: Kevin O'Neill | ISBN: 978-1-5638-9858-7 | Diamond Code: MAY118167 | Price: $16.99 | Format: TP

BATMAN:
EARTH ONE

GEOFF JOHNS REIMAGINES THE DARK KNIGHT'S ORIGIN STORY IN THIS #1 *NEW YORK TIMES* BESTSELLER

"This isn't just about capes and tights. This is stuff that, like the best of fiction, goes beyond the parameters of its particular genre." —*MTV Geek*

"Geoff Johns, the chief creative officer at DC Comics, has written us a Batman for Earth One that will knock your socks off." —*Huffington Post*

"Just when you thought there couldn't possibly be a fresh take on Batman, along come Johns and Frank to prove you extraordinarily wrong. Original, surprising and emotional, BATMAN: EARTH ONE is a must-read."
—Damon Lindelof (Co-creator and Executive Producer of *Lost*)

Batman is not a hero. He is just a man. Fallible, vulnerable and angry.

In Gotham City where friend and foe are indistinguishable, Bruce Wayne's path toward becoming the Dark Knight is riddled with more obstacles than ever before. Focused on punishing his parents' true killer, and the corrupt police who allowed them to go free, Bruce Wayne's thirst for vengeance fuels his mad crusade and no one, not even Alfred, can stop him.

In this #1 *New York Times* bestseller, writer Geoff Johns and artist Gary Frank reimagine a new mythology for the Dark Knight, where the familiar is no longer the expected in this original graphic novel.

BATMAN: EARTH ONE

Writer: Geoff Johns | Artist: Gary Frank | ISBN: 978-1-4012-3208-5 | Diamond Code: MAR120234 | Price: $22.99 | Format: HC

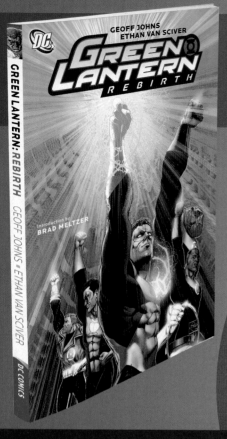

GREEN LANTERN:
REBIRTH
A HAL JORDAN
FOR A NEW GENERATION

"An EPIC BLOCKBUSTER." —CNN

"This is comic book storytelling at its ABSOLUTE FINEST." —IGN

"Readers will thrill at seeing one of the DC Universe's best mythologies begin to return to its former glory."
—*Washington Post*

Hal Jordan was the greatest Green Lantern of them all, until his shocking fall from grace. After years away, the battle for Emerald Warrior's soul has begun in earnest, with an alien evil threatening to consume the galaxy. As the other heroes on Earth (and beyond) attempt to save the Earth, several strive to bring back their fallen friend into the land of the living.

GREEN LANTERN: REBIRTH is the best-selling graphic novel that relaunches one of the DC Comics' greatest heroes from writer Geoff Johns and artist Ethan Van Sciver.

GREEN LANTERN: REBIRTH

Writer: Geoff Johns | Artist: Ethan Van Sciver | ISBN: 978-1-4012-2755-5 | Diamond Code: FEB100185 | Price: $14.99 | Format: TP

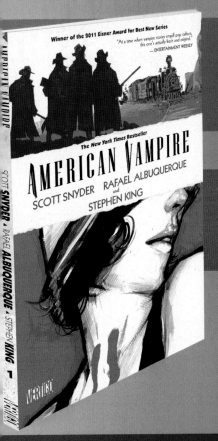

AMERICAN VAMPIRE
VOL.1

SCOTT SNYDER AND STEPHEN KING SET FIRE TO THE HORROR GENRE WITH A VISIONARY TAKE ON ONE OF POP CULTURE'S MOST INFAMOUS MONSTERS

"A rich, textured romp through vampire Americana, in such a fun way as to suggest the possibilities of this vehicle are as endless as the lives of the undead." —IGN

"Looking for a vampire story with some real bite? Then, boys and girls, Scott Snyder has a comic book for you." —*USA Weekend*

Everything you know about vampires has changed. The first bloodsucker conceived on American soil, Skinner Sweet is not your usual creature of the night. Stronger, fiercer, and powered by the sun, he is the first of a new breed: the American Vampire.

In this 2011 winner of the Eisner Award for Best New Series, comics superstar Scott Snyder and the master of horror Stephen King join forces for one of Vertigo's strongest—and most original—series ever.

AMERICAN VAMPIRE VOL. 1

Writers: Scott Snyder & Stephen King | Artist: Rafael Albuquerque | ISBN: 978-1-4012-2974-0 | Diamond Code: JUL110284 | Price: $19.99 | Format: TP

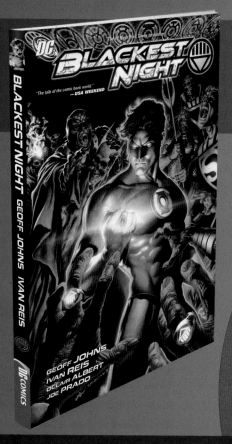

BLACKEST NIGHT

AGAINST AN ARMY OF UNDEAD BLACK LANTERNS—COMPOSED OF FRIEND AND FOE ALIKE—GREEN LANTERN AND EARTH'S HEROES MUST SAVE THE UNIVERSE FROM IMPENDING DARKNESS

"The talk of the comic book world."
—*USA Weekend*

"THRILLING and SHOCKING in equal measure .. reads like a movie—a movie filled with superheroes zombies, and those few poor saps caught in betwee. the two." —IGN

"The dead will rise. And that's good news for comic book readers in Space Sector 2814."
—*New York Daily News*

Across thousands of worlds, the dead have risen. These Black Lanterns, heroes and villains from beyond the grave have one purpose: extinguish all light—and life—in the universe.

While the Blackest Night consumes Earth's heroes, the seven corps empowered by the emotional spectrum—including Hal Jordan and the Green Lanterns—must end their war against each other, or bear witness to the end of creation. By the creative team of Geoff Johns and Ivan Reis, BLACKEST NIGHT is one of the great epics in the Green Lantern mythos!

BLACKEST NIGHT

Writer: Geoff Johns | Artists: Ivan Reis & others | ISBN: 978-1-4012-2953-5 | Diamond Code: APR110192 | Price: $19.99 | Format: TP

FINAL CRISIS

SUPERMAN, BATMAN AND THE REST OF THE JUSTICE LEAGUE FIGHT DARKSEID IN THE ULTIMATE BATTLE FOR THE FATE OF THE MULTIVERSE

"EPIC." —*Washington Post*

"The fertile mind of writer Grant Morrison ... this [is] THE EVENT TO TRUMP ALL EVENTS."
—*Entertainment Weekly*

"BEAUTIFUL." —*Publishers Weekly*

What happens when evil wins? That's the devastating question Superman, Batman, and the Justice League must face when Darkseid and his invading hordes win the war between light and dark. The fate of the universe is in jeopardy, and in order to see tomorrow, one of the world's greatest superheroes will pay the ultimate price.

Written by superstar creator Grant Morrison with stellar art from J.G. Jones, Carlos Pacheco and Doug Mahnke, this graphic novel is one of the most ambitious works in DC history.

FINAL CRISIS

Writer: Grant Morrison | Artists: J.G. Jones, Doug Mahnke & Carlos Pacheco | ISBN: 978-1-4012-2282-6 | Diamond Code: MAR100239 | Price: $19.99 | Format: TP

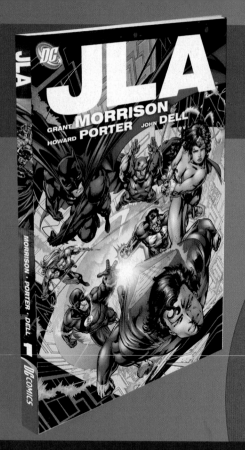

JLA VOL. 1
GRANT MORRISON RELAUNCHES THE GREATEST TEAM IN THE DC UNIVERSE WITH THE WORLD'S MOST POWERFUL HEROES

"[Grant Morrison is] comics' high shaman." —*Washington Post*

"Morrison's JLA is overloaded with cool moments, cooler lines, and that ever-present vibe of greatness we've come to expect from superhero team books. To this day fans are still citing this work as the 'model' for the JLA franchise." —*Newsarama*

Renegade angels, alien invaders and robot infiltrators. Sometimes, even the World's Greatest Superheroes face threats too great for one man ... or woman. DC's pantheon of champions—Superman, Batman, Wonder Woman, The Flash, Green Lantern, Aquaman, and Martian Manhunter—are finally united as the JLA.

Critically acclaimed writer Grant Morrison ushers in a brand-new era for DC's finest in this graphic novel that changed the dynamics of the 90s superhero.

JLA VOL. 1

Writer: Grant Morrison | Artists: Howard Porter & Oscar Jimenez | ISBN: 978-1-4012-3314-3 | Diamond Code: JUN110276 | Price: $19.99 | Format: TP

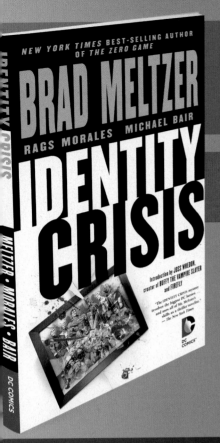

IDENTITY CRISIS
UNCOVER THE DC UNIVERSE'S DEADLIEST SECRET IN THIS ACCLAIMED STORY FROM *NEW YORK TIMES* BEST-SELLING NOVELIST BRAD MELTZER

"The IDENTITY CRISIS mystery involves the biggest DC heroes and will use all of Mr. Meltzer's skills as a thriller novelist." —*The New York Times*

"Meltzer shows that even superheroes have reasons to be afraid." —*SPIN Magazine*

"Meltzer deftly handles this foray into the question of how far the 'good guys' can go in questioning a 'bad guy.' One hopes that Meltzer enjoyed his stay in the comic book world enough to make a trip back someday." —*Chicago Sun-Times*

After a grisly murder rocks the DC Universe, the entire superhero community searches for the killer. But before the mystery is solved, a number of long-buried secrets will threaten to divide the Justice League.

New York Times best-selling novelist Brad Meltzer teams with critically acclaimed artist Rags Morales to unravel one of the most intimate and heartbreaking graphic novels ever.

IDENTITY CRISIS

Writer: Brad Meltzer | Artist: Rags Morales | ISBN: 978-1-4012-0458-7 | Diamond Code: AUG118125 | Price: $17.99 | Format: TP

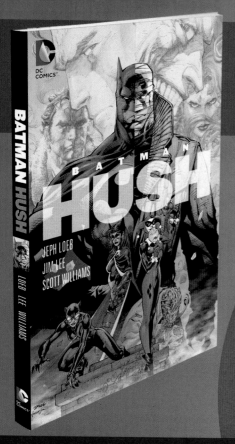

BATMAN: HUSH

BATMAN STALKS A NEW AND DEADLY VILLAIN WHO SEEMS TO KNOW MORE ABOUT BATMAN THAN ANYONE—HUSH!

"IT'S BEAUTIFUL STUFF. Catwoman has rarely looked so seductive, nor has Batman's heroic but fearsome image often been used so well. [Hush] make[s] readers look at Batman and his colleagues with a fresh, enthusiastic eye."
—*Publishers Weekly*

"Just might be [Jim Lee's] best work in his time at DC Comics." —IGN

Gotham City's worst criminals have emerged to throw Batman's life into utter chaos. However, these villains—Joker, Riddler, Ra's al Ghul, Clayface and others—are a part of a much more elaborate, sinister scheme to destroy the Dark Knight once and for all. Pushed past his breaking point, Batman will need to use more than the world's greatest detective skills to uncover the true mastermind behind this murderous plot before those closest to Bruce Wayne suffer the consequences.

In this truly unforgettable story by two of comics' top talents, writer Jeph Loeb and DC Co-Publisher Jim Lee presents the Caped Crusader's most personal case yet.

BATMAN: HUSH

Writer: Jeph Loeb | Artist: Jim Lee | ISBN: 978-1-4012-2317-5 | Diamond Code: MAY090178 | Price: $24.99 | Format: TP

JOKER

BRIAN AZZARELLO AND LEE BERMEJO'S ORIGINAL GRAPHIC NOVEL MASTERPIECE TRACES THE MOST VILE, DANGEROUS AND UNPREDICTABLE INMATE OF ARKHAM—THE JOKER!

"Disturbing, violent, oddly psychological and INSANELY WONDERFUL." —*USA Today*

"If you liked THE DARK KNIGHT, JOKER is a must-have for your bookshelf." —MTV.com

"A LITERARY ACHIEVEMENT that takes its place right alongside Alan Moore's BATMAN: THE KILLING JOKE." —IGN

The Joker has been mysteriously released from Arkham Asylum, and he's not too happy about what's happened to his town while he's been away. What follows is a harrowing night of revenge, murder and manic crime, as he brutally takes back his stolen assets from The Penguin, Riddler, Two-Face, Killer Croc, and, of course, The Batman.

Brian Azzarello brings all the visceral intensity and criminal insight to JOKER that has made his Vertigo graphic novel series *100 Bullets* one of the most critically acclaimed and award-winning comic series of this generation. With gorgeous illustrations by one of the industry's very best in Lee Bermejo, Batman's greatest foe takes center stage in this true *crime noir* novel—a harrowing journey into a city of rain-soaked streets, dirty sheets and nothing but bad choices.

JOKER

Writer: Brian Azzarello | Artist: Lee Bermejo | ISBN: 978-1-4012-1581-1 | Diamond Code: JUL080124 | Price: $19.99 | Format: HC

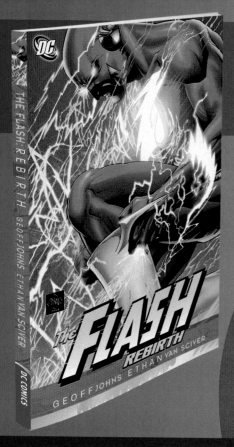

THE FLASH:
REBIRTH
AN EXPLOSIVE EPIC THAT REINTRODUCES THE NEWLY RETURNED BARRY ALLEN AS THE FLASH!

"IMPRESSIVE." —*MTV Splash Page*

"By weaving in CLEVER uses of continuity as well as the seemingly SINISTER energies of the Speed Force, I think the Flash couldn't be in better hands." —*Newsarama*

"THE FLASH: REBIRTH is writer Geoff Johns's terrific reboot of the Barry Allen Flash."
—*Entertainment Weekly*

Barry Allen—The Flash—died heroically defending the universe from a cosmic crisis and it made him a legend.

Now even as another crisis has brought Barry back to life, mysteries abound surrounding his return. Why was Barry able to escape the Speed Force—the extra-dimensional energy field that all speedsters draw from—when other heroes and villains were not? Most of all, who is it who brought Barry back to life ... and was The Flash reborn only so he could be destroyed once again?

THE FLASH: REBIRTH

Writer: Geoff Johns | Artist: Ethan Van Sciver | ISBN: 978-1-4012-3001-2 | Diamond Code: JAN110329 | Price: $14.99 | Format: TP

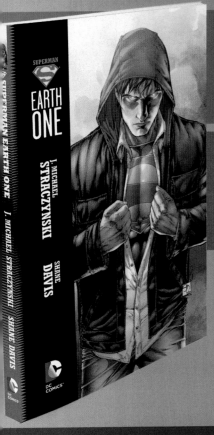

SUPERMAN:
EARTH ONE VOL.1
THE #1 *NEW YORK TIMES* BEST-SELLING ORIGINAL GRAPHIC NOVEL THAT REIMAGINES SUPERMAN AS A BROODING, RELUCTANT HERO IN MODERN-DAY METROPOLIS

"A Superman for a new generation.... J. Michael Straczynski and Shane Davis managed to breathe a new perspective into the character, full of all the classicism the character demands, but full of all the modernity required to make it fresh for a brand-new audience." —*Huffington Post*

"A modern, youthful take on the iconic superhero."—*USA Today*

"From its poignant domestic moments, delivered in mostly warm, fuzzy flashbacks, to its blockbuster battles, Straczynski's SUPERMAN: EARTH ONE renders like a feature film just waiting for adaptation."—*Wired*

Clark Kent is different. He can fly. He can see through walls, burn objects with his gaze. He is a man amongst mortals. But he is alone. Like most twenty-year-olds, he doesn't know what he wants to do with his life. After all, when you can do anything, the sky is the limit. But when the skies darken with ships from distant planets and the existence of Earth itself is threatened, Clark must make the most important decision of his life: To reveal himself to the world, or let everything die around him.

J. Michael Straczynski and Shane Davis modernize Superman for the 21st century in SUPERMAN: EARTH ONE in this #1 *New York Times* bestseller.

SUPERMAN: EARTH ONE VOL. 1

Writer: J. Michael Straczynski | Artist: Shane Davis | ISBN: 978-1-4012-2469-1 | Diamond Code: FEB130226 | Price: $12.99 | Format: TP

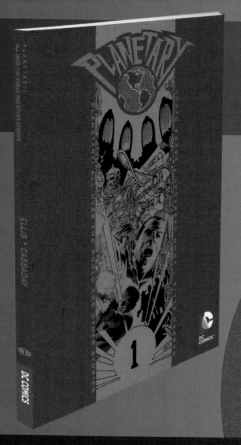

PLANETARY VOL. 1: ALL OVER THE WORLD AND OTHER STORIES

THE LANDMARK SERIES DETAILING THE ADVENTURES OF THE ARCHEOLOGISTS OF THE UNKNOWN, A GROUP TASKED WITH TRACKING DOWN FORGOTTEN HISTORIES OF CIVILIZATION

"PROVOCATIVE, eminently ADDICTIVE, and top of its class." —*Entertainment Weekly*

"[A] DARKLY WITTY, breathtakingly illustrated takes on familiar characters." —*The Onion/A.V. Club*

"Comic book storytelling rarely gets better than PLANETARY." —Craveonline.com

Planetary: A group tasked with tracking down evidence of super-human activity, paranormal secrets and forgotten histories of civilization. Three members, Elijah Snow, Jakita Wagner and The Drummer, form the organization's ground team, serving as archeologists of the unknown in a vast world of secrets.

Hailed as a timeless story that turns modern superhero convention on its head, genre-bending writer Warren Ellis and the amazing John Cassaday deliver PLANETARY.

PLANETARY VOL 1: ALL OVER THE WORLD AND OTHER STORIES

Writer: Warren Ellis | Artist: John Cassaday | ISBN: 978-1-5638-9648-4 | Diamond Code: FEB068129 | Price: $14.99 | Format: TP

WELCOME TO
THE NEW 52!
THE PLACE TO START

In September 2011, DC Entertainment embarked on an historic journey, one that would change the comic book industry forever. In 52 all-new #1 issues, the best creators in the business produced brand-new character origins, easy jumping-on points and stories that fit within the context of the 21st century. All these aspects came together to create a new mythology that paid homage to everything that's happened, while also laying the foundation for our rapidly changing future.

THIS IS THE BIGGEST EVENT IN COMIC BOOK HISTORY.
START AT THE BEGINNING.

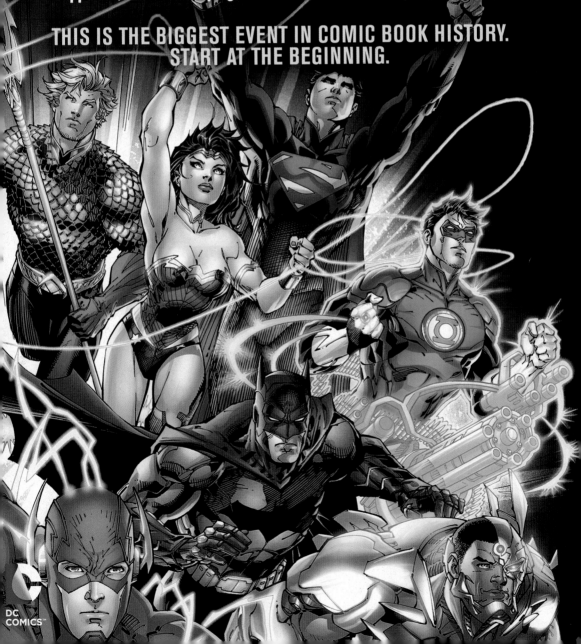

JUSTICE LEAGUE
VOL. 1: ORIGIN

GEOFF JOHNS AND JIM LEE UNITE FOR THE FIRST TIME TO LAUNCH THE BOLD NEW BEGINNING OF THE DC UNIVERSE'S PREMIER SUPER TEAM!

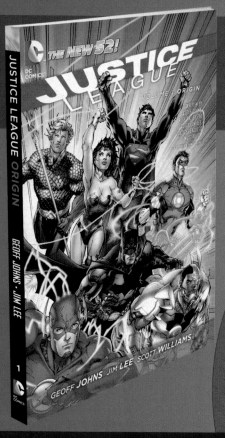

"A must-read." —*Complex Magazine*

"Writer Geoff Johns and artist Jim Lee toss you—and their heroes—into the action from the very start and don't put on the brakes. DC's über-creative team craft an inviting world for those who are trying out a comic for the first time." —*USA Today*

"Welcoming to new fans looking to get into superhero comics for the first time and old fans who gave up on the funny-books long ago." —*MTV Geek*

It's the dawn of a new age of superheroes, frightening to the world at large. Superman. Batman. The Flash. Wonder Woman. Green Lantern. Aquaman. Cyborg. Though young and inexperienced, brash and overconfident, each one alone is a powerful force in the battle of good against evil. Together, they may be the only thing on Earth that can stop the alien warlord Darkseid from claiming our planet as his own. Together they will become the Justice League!

JUSTICE LEAGUE VOL. 1: ORIGIN

Writer: Geoff Johns | Artist: Jim Lee | ISBN: 978-1-4012-3788-2 | Diamond Code: OCT120252 | Price: $16.99 | Format: TP

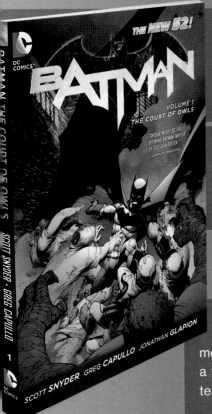

BATMAN
VOL. 1: THE COURT OF OWLS

A NEW ERA FOR THE DARK KNIGHT AND GOTHAM CITY BEGINS HERE IN THIS #1 *NEW YORK TIMES* BESTSELLER!

"A stunning debut.... Snyder knows these characters, sets up an intriguing mystery, and delivers some action that Capullo realizes stunningly. This is definitely in the top rank of the revamp."
—*The Onion/A.V. Club*

"Snyder might be the defining Batman writer of our generation." —*Complex Magazine*

"[Writer Scott Snyder] pulls from the oldest aspects of the Batman myth, combines it with sinister comic elements from the series' best period, and gives the whole thing a terrific forward-spin by setting up an honest-to-gosh mystery for Batman to solve." —*Entertainment Weekly*

IGN's Best Comic Book series of 2012!

Batman has heard tales of Gotham City's Court of Owls: That the members of this powerful cabal are the true rulers of Gotham. The Dark Knight dismissed the stories as rumors and old wives' tales. Gotham was *his* city. Until now.

A brutal assassin is sinking his razor-sharp talons into the city's best and brightest, as well as its most dangerous and deadly. If the dark legends are true, his masters are more powerful predators than the Batman could ever imagine.

BATMAN VOL. 1: THE COURT OF OWLS

Writer: Scott Snyder | Artist: Greg Capullo | ISBN: 978-1-4012-3542-0 | Diamond Code: DEC120323 | Price: $16.99 | Format: TP

ANIMAL MAN VOL. 1: THE HUNT

Writer: Jeff Lemire | Artist: Travel Foreman
ISBN: 978-1-4012-3507-9 | Diamond Code: FEB120247 | Price: $14.99 | Format: TP

Buddy Baker has gone from "super" man to family man—but is he strong enough to hold his family together when his young daughter starts to manifest her own dangerous powers?

AQUAMAN VOL. 1: THE TRENCH

Writer: Geoff Johns | Artist: Ivan Reis
ISBN: 978-1-4012-3710-3 | Diamond Code: FEB130206 | Price $14.99 | Format: TP

Superstar writer Geoff Johns re-teams with artist Ivan Reis to relaunch Aquaman as one of the most powerful and important heroes of the DC Universe.

ALL-STAR WESTERN VOL. 1: GUNS AND GOTHAM

Writers: Jimmy Palmiotti and Justin Gray | Artist: Moritat
ISBN: 978-1-4012-3709-7 | Diamond Code: JUL120213 | Price: $16.99 | Format: TP

Jonah Hex teams with Amadeus Arkham to track down a serial killer and search for a missing child in Gotham City during the era of the Wild West.

BATGIRL VOL. 1: THE DARKEST REFLECTION

Writer: Gail Simone | Artist: Ardian Syaf
ISBN: 978-1-4012-3814-8 | Diamond Code: NOV120262 | Price: $14.99 | Format: TP

Barbara Gordon finally returns as Batgirl in this #1 *New York Times* bestseller.

BATMAN: DETECTIVE COMICS VOL. 1: FACES OF DEATH

Writer: Tony S. Daniel | Artist: Tony S. Daniel
ISBN: 978-1-4012-3467-6 | Diamond Code: FEB120245 | Price: $16.99 | Format: TP

Writer/artist Tony S. Daniel's take on Batman's infamous rogues' gallery.

BATMAN: THE DARK KNIGHT VOL. 1: KNIGHT TERRORS

Writers: David Finch & Paul Jenkins | Artist: David Finch
ISBN: 978-1-4012-3543-7 | Diamond Code: JUN120234 | Price: $24.99 | Format: HC

The Dark Knight faces Gotham's supernatural threats.

BATMAN & ROBIN VOL. 1: BORN TO KILL

Writer: Peter J. Tomasi | Artist: Patrick Gleason
ISBN: 978-1-4012-3487-4 | Diamond Code: MAR120241 | Price: $24.99 | Format: HC

Damian Wayne, Batman's long-lost son, takes over the mantle of the
Boy Wonder.

BATWING VOL. 1: THE LOST KINGDOM

Writer: Judd Winick | Artist: Ben Oliver
ISBN: 978-1-4012-3476-8 | Diamond Code: APR120246 | Price: $14.99 | Format: TP

Spinning out of the pages of Batman, Incorporated, introducing Africa's
greatest hero.

BATWOMAN VOL. 1: HYDROLOGY

Writers: J.H. Williams III & W. Haden Blackman | Artist: J.H. Williams III
ISBN: 978-1-4012-3784-4 | Diamond Code: OCT120253 | Price: $14.99 | Format: TP

J.H. Williams III's beautiful and complex series about Gotham's newest protector
in this #1 *New York Times* bestseller.

BIRDS OF PREY VOL. 1: TROUBLE IN MIND

Writer: Duane Swierczynski | Artists: Jesús Saíz & Javier Pina
ISBN: 978-1-4012-3699-1 | Diamond Code: JUN120236 | Price: $14.99 | Format: TP

The most dangerous women of the DCU tackle crime on the streets of Gotham.

BLACKHAWKS VOL. 1: THE GREAT LEAP FORWARD

Writer: Mike Costa | Artists: Cafu & Graham Nolan
ISBN: 978-1-4012-3714-1 | Diamond Code: AUG120247 | Price: $16.99 | Format: TP

The world's foremost covert ops team face threats both foreign and domestic ...
and from within.

BLUE BEETLE VOL.1: METAMORPHOSIS

Writer: Tony Bedard | Artist: Ig Guara
ISBN: 978-1-4012-3713-4 | Diamond Code: AUG120246 | Price: $14.99 | Format: TP

Teenager Jaime Reyés finds himself saddled with strange alien armor that
transforms him into Blue Beetle.

CAPTAIN ATOM VOL. 1: EVOLUTION

Writer: J.T. Krul | Artist: Freddie Williams II
ISBN: 978-1-4012-3715-8 | Diamond Code: AUG120250 | Price: $14.99 | Format: TP

Captain Nathaniel Adam's incredible new powers will either destroy the world or save it.

CATWOMAN VOL. 1: THE GAME

Writer: Judd Winick | Artist: Guillem March
ISBN: 978-1-4012-3464-5| Diamond Code: FEB120248 | Price: $14.99 | Format: TP

Catwoman Selina Kyle is addicted to stealing ... and Batman.

DC UNIVERSE PRESENTS VOL. 1 FEATURING DEADMAN & THE CHALLENGERS OF THE UNKNOWN

Writers: Paul Jenkins & Dan DiDio | Artists: Bernard Chang & Jerry Ordway
ISBN: 978-1-4012-3716-5 | Diamond Code: AUG120251 | Price: $16.99 | Format: TP

This graphic novel spotlights DC's strangest heroes.

DEATHSTROKE VOL. 1: LEGACY

Writer: Kyle Higgins | Artist: Joe Bennett
ISBN: 978-1-4012-3481-2 | Diamond Code: MAY120282 | Price: $16.99 | Format: TP

Mercenary Slade Wilson's life is on the line ... and so is his reputation.

DEMON KNIGHTS VOL. 1: SEVEN AGAINST THE DARK

Writer: Paul Cornell | Artist: Diogenes Neves
ISBN: 978-1-4012-3472-0 | Diamond Code: APR120247 | Price: $14.99 | Format: TP

The medieval Justice League.

THE FLASH VOL. 1: MOVE FORWARD

Writers: Francis Manapul & Brian Buccellato | Artist: Francis Manapul
ISBN: 978-1-4012-3553-6 | Diamond Code: JUL120209 | Price: $24.99 | Format: HC

The Fastest Man Alive returns as Central City's greatest protector.

GREEN LANTERN
VOL. 1: SINESTRO

GEOFF JOHNS AND DOUG MAHNKE LIGHT UP THE COMIC SKIES WITH THE RING-SLINGING CORPS AND THEIR NEWEST MEMBER: SINESTRO!

"Geoff Johns has turned Sinestro, Green Lantern's former enemy, into a three-dimensional character ... fascinating." —*The New York Times*

"It looks good and the story zips along. Sinestro is my favorite sort of villain: a bad guy who doesn't think he's a bad guy."—*The Onion/A.V. Club*

"A cosmic/sci-fi/space-opera that has tons of action and an emotional anchor in Hal Jordan.... This is a perfect place for people wary of the Green Lantern to start reading his adventures in order to see just how dynamic his world really is." —*Complex Magazine*

Hal Jordan, once considered the greatest Green Lantern in the universe, is being given the chance to soar once more by rejoining the intergalactic Green Lantern Corps. There's just one catch: This Green Lantern ring is coming from Sinestro, one of the greatest villains the universe has ever known—and a controversial addition to the Corps. If Hal accepts Sinestro's offer, it means accepting Sinestro's terms ... and that means rescuing the rogue Lantern's home planet from the evil army of murderers that Sinestro himself assembled!

GREEN LANTERN VOL. 1: SINESTRO

Writer: Geoff Johns | Artist: Doug Mahnke | ISBN: 978-1-4012-3455-3 | Diamond Code: OCT120257 | Price: $14.99 | Format: TP

FRANKENSTEIN, AGENT OF S.H.A.D.E. VOL. 1: WAR OF THE MONSTERS

Writer: Jeff Lemire | Artist: Alberto Ponticelli
ISBN: 978-1-4012-3471-3 | Diamond Code: MAR120244 | Price: $14.99 | Format: TP

Jeff Lemire presents Frankenstein as you've never seen him before!

THE FURY OF FIRESTORM: THE NUCLEAR MEN VOL. 1: GOD PARTICLE

Writers: Gail Simone & Ethan Van Sciver | Artist: Yildiray Cinar
ISBN: 978-1-4012-3700-4 | Diamond Code: JUN120237 | Price: $14.99 | Format: TP

Two teenagers with nothing in common find themselves bonded in the body of the atom-smashing Firestorm.

GREEN ARROW VOL. 1: THE MIDAS TOUCH

Writers: J.T. Krul & Keith Giffen | Artists: Dan Jurgens & George Pérez
ISBN: 978-1-4012-3486-7 | Diamond Code: FEB120249 | Price: $14.99 | Format: TP

Reimagines the sharp-shooting, emerald-clad DC hero Oliver Queen, also known as Green Arrow!

GREEN LANTERN CORPS VOL. 1: FEARSOME

Writer: Peter J. Tomasi | Artist: Fernando Pasarin
ISBN: 978-1-4012-3701-1 | Diamond Code: MAY120279 | Price: $22.99 | Format: HC

The intergalactic peace-keeping corps face a threat from the Guardians' past.

GREEN LANTERN: NEW GUARDIANS VOL. 1: THE RING BEARER

Writer: Tony Bedard | Artist: Tyler Kirkham
ISBN: 978-1-4012-3707-3 | Diamond Code: JUN120235 | Price: $22.99 | Format: HC

Spinning out of *Green Lantern*, members from all the various Lantern Corps tenuously unite into their own team of renegades.

GRIFTER VOL. 1: MOST WANTED

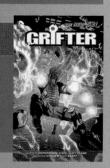

Writer: Nathan Edmondson | Artist: Cafu & Scott Clark
ISBN: 978-1-4012-3497-3 | Diamond Code: APR120248 | Price: $16.99 | Format: TP

Grifter's first starring role in his own series!

HAWK AND DOVE VOL. 1: FIRST STRIKES

Writers: Sterling Gates & Rob Liefeld | Artist: Rob Liefeld
ISBN: 978-1-4012-3498-0 | Diamond Code: MAY120281 | Price: $16.99 | Format: TP

The forces of order and chaos fight against evil ... if they don't kill each other first.

I, VAMPIRE VOL. 1: TAINTED LOVE

Writer: Joshua Hale Fialkov | Artist: Andrea Sorrentino
ISBN: 978-1-4012-3687-8 | Diamond Code: JUL120212 | Price: $14.99 | Format: TP

Vampire Andrew Bennett battles a horde of bloodsuckers led by his star-crossed lover Mary, Queen of Blood.

JUSTICE LEAGUE DARK VOL. 1: IN THE DARK

Writer: Peter Milligan | Artist: Mikel Janin
ISBN: 978-1-4012-3704-2 | Diamond Code: JUL120211 | Price: $14.99 | Format: TP

John Constantine leads a ragtag group of heroes against the world's most dangerous supernatural threats.

JUSTICE LEAGUE INTERNATIONAL VOL. 1: THE SIGNAL MASTERS

Writer: Dan Jurgens | Artist: Aaron Lopresti
ISBN: 978-1-4012-3534-5 | Diamond Code: FEB120250 | Price: $14.99 | Format: TP

The UN's answer to the Justice League battle against the Signal Masters.

LEGION LOST VOL. 1: RUN FROM TOMORROW

Writer: Fabian Nicieza | Artist: Pete Woods
ISBN: 978-1-4012-3703-5 | Diamond Code: JUN120238 | Price: $14.99 | Format: TP

Seven teenaged heroes from the future must find their way back to their own time.

LEGION OF SUPER-HEROES VOL. 1: HOSTILE WORLD

Writer: Paul Levitz | Artist: Francis Portella
ISBN: 978-1-4012-3501-7 | Diamond Code: MAR120246 | Price: $14.99 | Format: TP

The 31st Century super-team faces their gravest threat yet.

MEN OF WAR VOL. 1: UNEASY COMPANY

Writer: Ivan Brandon | Artist: Tom Derenick
ISBN: 978-1-4012-3499-7 | Diamond Code: APR120249 | Price: $19.99 | Format: TP

The grandson of legendary war hero Sgt. Rock leads the Easy Company into war.

MISTER TERRIFIC VOL. 1: MIND GAMES

Writer: Eric Wallace | Artist: Gianluca Gugliotta
ISBN: 978-1-4012-3500-0 | Diamond Code: MAR120247 | Price: $16.99 | Format: TP

Can the world's smartest man outwit the gravest threats in the cosmos?

NIGHTWING VOL. 1: TRAPS AND TRAPEZES

Writers: Kyle Higgins | Artist: Eddy Barrows
ISBN: 978-1-4012-3705-9 | Diamond Code: JUL120214 | Price: $14.99 | Format: TP

Dick Grayson flies high once more as Nightwing.

O.M.A.C. VOL. 1: OMACTIVATE!

Writer: Dan DiDio | Artist: Keith Giffen
ISBN: 978-1-4012-3482-9 | Diamond Code: MAY120283 | Price: $16.99 | Format: TP

Kevin Kho is unwillingly transformed into an unstoppable war machine called O.M.A.C.

RED HOOD AND THE OUTLAWS VOL. 1: REDEMPTION

Writer: Scott Lobdell | Artist: Kenneth Rocafort
ISBN: 978-1-4012-3712-7 | Diamond Code: AUG120248 | Price: $14.99 | Format: TP

Former Robin Jason Todd finds himself in an unlikely partnership with fellow misfits Arsenal and the exiled alien princess Starfire.

RED LANTERNS VOL. 1: BLOOD AND RAGE

Writer: Peter Milligan | Artist: Ed Benes
ISBN: 978-1-4012-3491-1 | Diamond Code: MAR120243 | Price: $14.99 | Format: TP

Atrocitus, leader of the Red Lanterns, wreaks fiery vengeance on those who prey on the innocent.

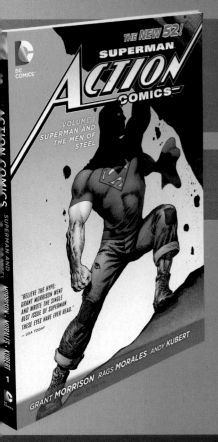

SUPERMAN:
ACTION COMICS VOL. 1:
SUPERMAN AND THE MEN OF STEEL

WRITER GRANT MORRISON LAYS DOWN YET ANOTHER INDUSTRY
BENCHMARK WITH HIS TAKE ON A YOUNG MAN OF STEEL

"Believe the hype: Grant Morrison went and wrote the single best issue of Superman these eyes have ever read." —*USA Today*

"A ripping read."
—*Entertainment Weekly*

"It's fresh air. I like this all-too-human Superman, and I think a lot of you will too."
—*Scripps Howard News Service*

Five years ago, before the superheroes took to the skies and changed life on Earth forever, one young hero dared to clean up the once-great city of Metropolis. A juggernaut of justice in jeans and a t-shirt.... It's SUPERMAN!

But the forces of fear are fighting back. Brilliant businessman Lex Luthor is out to crack the secrets of this alien interloper by any means necessary. The terrified military is ready to unleash its own super-weapon, custom-made to take the Last Son of Krypton down.

SUPERMAN: ACTION COMICS VOL. 1: SUPERMAN AND THE MEN OF STEEL

Writer: Grant Morrison | Artists: Rags Morales & Andy Kubert | ISBN: 978-1-4012-3547-5 | Diamond Code: FEB130215 | Price: $16.99 | Format: TP

RESURRECTION MAN VOL. 1: DEAD AGAIN

Writers: Andy Lanning & Dan Abnett | Artist: Fernando Dagnino
ISBN: 978-1-4012-3529-1 | Diamond Code: MAY120284 | Price: $14.99 | Format: TP

Every time Mitch Shelley dies, he comes back to life with new powers.

THE SAVAGE HAWKMAN VOL. 1: DARKNESS RISING

Writers: Tony S. Daniel & James Bonny | Artist: Philip Tan
ISBN: 978-1-4012-3706-6 | Diamond Code: JUL120215 | Price: $16.99 | Format: TP

Carter Hall takes to the skies in an effort to uncover the secrets of his past.

STATIC SHOCK VOL. 1: SUPERCHARGED

Writers: Scott McDaniel & John Rozum | Artist: Scott McDaniel
ISBN: 978-1-4012-3484-3 | Diamond Code: MAR120245 | Price: $16.99 | Format: TP

Get a jolt with New York City's most electrifying new hero.

STORMWATCH VOL. 1: THE DARK SIDE

Writer: Paul Cornell | Artist: Miguel Sepulveda
ISBN: 978-1-4012-3483-6 | Diamond Code: FEB120251 | Price: $14.99 | Format: TP

The world's most secret organization of superheroes protects the planet from inter-dimensional harm.

SUICIDE SQUAD VOL. 1: KICKED IN THE TEETH

Writer: Adam Glass | Artists: Federico Dallocchio & Clayton Henry
ISBN: 978-1-4012-3544-4 | Diamond Code: APR120250 | Price: $14.99 | Format: TP

A band of former super-villains are recruited by a shadowy government agency for missions so dangerous, it's suicide.

SUPERBOY VOL. 1: INCUBATION

Writer: Scott Lobdell | Artist: R.B. Silva
ISBN: 978-1-4012-3485-0 | Diamond Code: MAY120285 | Price: $14.99 | Format: TP

A secret organization called N.O.W.H.E.R.E. creates their own teenage Kryptonian, but for what nefarious purpose?

SUPERGIRL VOL. 1: LAST DAUGHTER OF KRYPTON

Writers: Michael Green & Mike Johnson | Artist: Mahmud Asrar
ISBN: 978-1-4012-3680-9 | Diamond Code: JUL120216 | Price: $14.99 | Format: TP

Superman's teenaged cousin mysteriously crash-lands on earth decades after the destruction of Krypton.

SUPERMAN VOL. 1: WHAT PRICE TOMORROW?

Writer: George Pérez | Artists: Jesús Merino & Nicola Scott
ISBN: 978-1-4012-3468-3 | Diamond Code: JUL120210 | Price: $22.99 | Format: HC

In a world that fears him, Superman must continue to safeguard Metropolis from threats that he himself has created.

SWAMP THING VOL. 1: RAISE THEM BONES

Writer: Scott Snyder | Artist: Yanick Paquette
ISBN: 978-1-4012-3462-1 | Diamond Code: MAY120280 | Price: $14.99 | Format: TP

One of the world's most iconic characters returns to the heart of the DC Universe!

TEEN TITANS VOL. 1: IT'S OUR RIGHT TO FIGHT

Writer: Scott Lobdell | Artist: Brett Booth
ISBN: 978-1-4012-3698-4 | Diamond Code: JUN120239 | Price: $14.99 | Format: TP

Scott Lobdell and Brett Booth launch an all-new Teen Titans into new and action-packed adventures!

VOODOO VOL. 1: WHAT LIES BENEATH

Writers: Ron Marz & Joshua Williamson | Artist: Sami Basri
ISBN: 978-1-4012-3561-1 | Diamond Code: JUN120240 | Price: $14.99 | Format: TP

Priscilla Kitaen is Voodoo, whose secret mission will either destroy the planet— or save it!

WONDER WOMAN VOL. 1: BLOOD

Writer: Brian Azzarello | Artists: Cliff Chiang & Tony Akins
ISBN: 978-1-4012-3562-8 | Diamond Code: OCT120256 | Price: $14.99 | Format: TP

Superheroics and ancient myth meet, as critically acclaimed writer Brian Azzarello teams with Cliff Chiang and Tony Akins to begin a new chapter for the Amazon Princess.

As a child, Bruce Wayne helplessly watched as his parents were brutally murdered in front of him. From that day forth, Bruce vowed to wage a one-man war on crime, donning the cape and the cowl to become Batman.

Created by Bob Kane in 1939, the Dark Knight has become a fixture in popular culture the world over.

BATMAN: YEAR ONE

Writer: Frank Miller | Artist: David Mazzucchelli
ISBN: 978-1-4012-0752-6 | Diamond Code: OCT060163 | Price: $14.99 | Format: TP

Frank Miller's genre-defining graphic novel detailing a rookie Dark Knight's first year in Gotham City.

BATMAN: THE LONG HALLOWEEN

Writer: Jeph Loeb | Artist: Tim Sale
ISBN: 978-1-4012-3259-7 | Diamond Code: JUL110251 | Price: $24.99 | Format: TP

A Batman murder mystery written by Jeph Loeb with art by Tim Sale, set during the Dark Knight's early days as he must race against the calendar to discover the identity of the serial killer Holiday.

BATMAN: DARK VICTORY

Writer: Jeph Loeb | Artist: Tim Sale
ISBN: 978-1-5638-9868-6 | Diamond Code: MAR058151 | Price: $19.99 | Format: TP

In this sequel to *Batman: The Long Halloween*, Batman faces another seemingly unsolvable mystery, as the Hangman runs through a murder spree in Gotham City.

BATMAN: ARKHAM ASYLUM

Writer: Grant Morrison | Artist: Dave McKean
ISBN: 978-1-4012-0425-9 | Diamond Code: AUG050185 | Price: $17.99 | Format: TP

Grant Morrison and Dave McKean's psychological horror story from Arkham Asylum, home to Gotham City's most deranged super-criminals.

FOR MATURE READERS

BATMAN: THE KILLING JOKE

Writer: Alan Moore | Artist: Brian Bolland
ISBN: 978-1-4012-1667-2 | Diamond Code: NOV070226 | Price: $17.99 | Format: HC

The Joker, Batman's greatest adversary, in his definitive origin story by Alan Moore with breathtaking art by Brian Bolland.

FOR MATURE READERS

BATMAN: KNIGHTFALL VOL. 1

Writer: Various | Artist: Various
ISBN: 978-1-4012-3379-2 | Diamond Code: JAN120303 | Price: $29.99 | Format: TP

Batman's entire rogues' gallery is freed from Arkham Asylum by the villainous Bane, who tests the Dark Knight mentally and physically as never before.

BATMAN: HUSH

Writer: Jeph Loeb | Artist: Jim Lee
ISBN: 978-1-4012-2317-5 | Diamond Code: MAY090178 | Price: $24.99 | Format: TP

The all-star team of Jeph Loeb and Jim Lee trace the tale of Batman as he seeks to stop a new and deadly villain who seems to know more about Batman than anyone—Hush!

BATMAN: UNDER THE RED HOOD

Writer: Judd Winick | Artist: Doug Mahnke
ISBN: 978-1-4012-3145-3 | Diamond Code: MAY110241 | Price: $29.99 | Format: TP

The Red Hood returns to Gotham City and his shocking actions—as well as his identity—will change Batman forever.

BATMAN AND SON

Writer: Grant Morrison | Artist: Andy Kubert
ISBN: 978-1-4012-1241-4 | Diamond Code: FEB128079 | Price: $16.99 | Format: TP

In Grant Morrison's opening arc on his epic Batman run, Bruce Wayne discovers that he's sired a son, but will he be able to save Damian Wayne, or fall victim to his own son's murderous nature?

BATMAN: R.I.P.

Writer: Grant Morrison | Artist: Tony S. Daniel
ISBN: 978-1-4012-2576-6 | Diamond Code: MAR100237 | Price: $14.99 | Format: TP

Grant Morrison continues his grand Batman storyline, pitting the Dark Knight against the Black Glove in a prelude to *Final Crisis*.

BATMAN & ROBIN VOL. 1: BATMAN REBORN

Writer: Grant Morrison | Artists: Frank Quitely & Philip Tan
ISBN: 978-1-4012-2987-0 | Diamond Code: DEC100246 | Price: $14.99 | Format: TP

The dynamic duo is reborn, with Dick Grayson donning the cowl along with new Robin Damian Wayne.

BATMAN: THE BLACK MIRROR

Writer: Scott Snyder | Artists: Francesco Francavilla & Jock
ISBN: 978-1-4012-3207-8 | Diamond Code: NOV120268 | Price: $16.99 | Format: TP

The past comes back to haunt Commissioner Gordon and Batman by way of a diabolical murder mystery, in this dark graphic novel that launched writer Scott Snyder into superstardom.

BATMAN INCORPORATED VOL. 1

Writer: Grant Morrison | Artist: Yanick Paquette
ISBN: 978-1-4012-3827-8 | Diamond Code: OCT120258 | Price: $19.99 | Format: TP

Batman deputizes different "Batmen" in nations around the globe, creating the indomitable Batman, Incorporated.

BATMAN VOL. 1: THE COURT OF OWLS

Writer: Scott Snyder | Artist: Greg Capullo
ISBN: 978-1-4012-3542-0 | Diamond Code: DEC120323 | Price: $16.99 | Format: TP

A new era for The Dark Knight and Gotham City begins here from writer Scott Snyder and artist Greg Capullo, as Batman and the Bat-Family continue their quest to protect the people of Gotham.

BATMAN: DETECTIVE COMICS VOL. 1: FACES OF DEATH

Writer: Tony S. Daniel | Artist: Tony S. Daniel
ISBN: 978-1-4012-3467-6 | Diamond Code: JAN130296 | Price: $16.99 | Format: TP

DC's flagship title re-launches for the first time ever, featuring Batman adventures from the acclaimed Tony S. Daniel!

BATMAN: THE DARK KNIGHT VOL. 1: KNIGHT TERRORS

Writers: David Finch & Paul Jenkins | Artist: David Finch
ISBN: 978-1-4012-3543-7 | Diamond Code: JUN120234 | Price: $24.99 | Format: HC

Superstar artist David Finch returns to Gotham as Batman must delve into the more supernatural and esoteric areas of Gotham City!

BATMAN & ROBIN VOL. 1: BORN TO KILL

Writer: Peter J. Tomasi | Artist: Patrick Gleason
ISBN: 978-1-4012-3487-4 | Diamond Code: MAR120241 | Price: $24.99 | Format: HC

The Dynamic Duo toil as father and son in this series by the creative team behind the *Green Lantern Corps*—Peter Tomasi and Patrick Gleason.

BATMAN: EARTH ONE

Writer: Geoff Johns | Artist: Gary Frank
ISBN: 978-1-4012-3208-5 | Diamond Code: MAR120234 | Price: $22.99 | Format: HC

Geoff Johns re-imagines the Dark Knight's origin story in this #1 *New York Times* bestseller.

BATMAN: THE DARK KNIGHT RETURNS

Writer: Frank Miller | Artist: Frank Miller
ISBN: 978-1-5638-9342-1 | Diamond Code: NOV118095 | Price: $19.99 | Format: TP

Frank Miller's classic and gritty take on the return of Gotham's hero.

BATMAN: THE DARK KNIGHT STRIKES AGAIN

Writer: Frank Miller | Artist: Frank Miller
ISBN: 978-1-5638-9929-4 | Diamond Code: FEB058404 | Price: $19.99 | Format: TP

The sequel to *Batman: The Dark Knight Returns*, in which Batman must come back once more to save a rapidly decaying world.

Rocketed to Earth from the dying planet Krypton, baby Kal-El
was raised on Earth by a kindly farming couple. Clark Kent, as
he was renamed, grew up and discovered that he had extraordinary powers far exceeding everyone around him. Combined
with the strong moral values his adoptive parents instilled in
him, he became Superman. Created by Jerry Siegel and Joe
Shuster, the Man of Steel was the first—and now most recognized—super-hero in pop culture.

SUPERMAN CHRONICLES VOL. 1

Writer: Jerry Siegel | Artist: Joe Shuster
ISBN: 978-1-4012-0764-9 | Diamond Code: NOV050250 | Price: $14.99 | Format: TP

The first adventures of the Man of Steel.

SUPERMAN: WHATEVER HAPPENED TO THE MAN OF TOMORROW?

Writer: Alan Moore | Artists: Curt Swan & George Pérez
ISBN: 978-1-4012-2731-9| Diamond Code: APR100219 | Price: $14.99 | Format: TP

Alan Moore's quintessential Superman story.

SUPERMAN: MAN OF STEEL VOL. 1

Writer: John Byrne | Artist: John Byrne
ISBN: 978-0-9302-8928-7 | Diamond Code: JUL058226 | Price: $14.99 | Format: TP

The first re-telling of Superman's epic origin!

SUPERMAN: FOR ALL SEASONS

Writer: Jeph Loeb | Artist: Tim Sale
ISBN: 978-1-5638-9529-6 | Diamond Code: FEB068194 | Price: $17.99 | Format: TP

The tale of Clark Kent's transformation from country boy to Metropolis Superman as told by the acclaimed duo of Jeph Loeb and Tim Sale.

SUPERMAN: THE DEATH OF SUPERMAN

Writer: Various | Artist: Various
ISBN: 978-1-4012-4182-7 | Diamond Code: OCT120269 | Price: $14.99 | Format: TP

The story that shocked the world! Superman pays the ultimate price to stop the killing machine Doomsday.

SUPERMAN/BATMAN: PUBLIC ENEMIES VOL. 1

Writer: Jeph Loeb | Artist: Ed McGuinness
ISBN: 978-1-4012-0220-0 | Diamond Code: JUL090239 | Price: $14.99 | Format: TP

Superman and Batman team up to combat the machinations of President of the United States Lex Luthor in this graphic novel by Jeph Loeb and Ed McGuinness.

LUTHOR

Writer: Brian Azzarello | Artist: Lee Bermejo
ISBN: 978-1-4012-2930-6 | Diamond Code: JUN100212 | Price: $19.99 | Format: HC

The all-star team of Brian Azzarello and Lee Bermejo explores the mind of the Superman's greatest villain Lex Luthor.

SUPERMAN: FOR TOMORROW

Writer: Brian Azzarello | Artist: Jim Lee
ISBN: 978-1-4012-3780-6 | Diamond Code: NOV120270 | Price: $24.99 | Format: TP

A cataclysmic event has caused half of the Earth's population to disappear and no one is left unaffected, including Superman in this graphic novel by the superstar team of Jim Lee and Brian Azzarello.

SUPERMAN: SECRET ORIGIN

Writer: Geoff Johns | Artist: Gary Frank
ISBN: 978-1-4012-3299-3 | Diamond Code: SEP110188 | Price: $19.99 | Format: TP

The origin of Superman as told by the *New York Times* best-selling team of Geoff Johns and Gary Frank.

SUPERMAN: LAST SON OF KRYPTON

Writers: Geoff Johns & Richard Donner | Artists: Adam Kubert & Gary Frank
ISBN: 978-1-4012-3779-0 | Diamond Code: OCT120270 | Price: $19.99 | Format: TP

Superman director Richard Donner and Geoff Johns pit the Man of Steel against General Zod and Brainiac in these stories illustrated by Adam Kubert and Gary Frank.

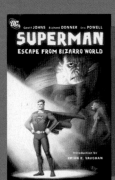

SUPERMAN: ESCAPE FROM BIZARRO WORLD

Writers: Geoff Johns & Richard Donner | Artist: Eric Powell
ISBN: 978-1-4012-2033-4 | Diamond Code: FEB090217 | Price: $14.99 | Format: TP

Superman travels to the backwards planet Bizarro World.

SUPERMAN AND THE LEGION OF SUPER-HEROES

Writer: Geoff Johns | Artist: Gary Frank
ISBN: 978-1-4012-1904-8 | Diamond Code: APR090217 | Price: $14.99 | Format: TP

The first meeting between Superman and the Legion of Super-Heroes.

SUPERMAN: THE BLACK RING VOL. 1

Writer: Paul Cornell | Artist: Pete Woods
ISBN: 978-1-4012-3034-0 | Diamond Code: NOV110203 | Price: $14.99 | Format: TP

To gain the power he craves and overtake Superman as the planet's most powerful being, Lex Luthor must unlock the power of the Black Lantern rings.

SUPERMAN: ACTION COMICS VOL. 1: SUPERMAN AND THE MEN OF STEEL

Writer: Grant Morrison | Artists: Rags Morales & Andy Kubert
ISBN: 978-1-4012-3547-5 | Diamond Code: FEB130215 | Price: $16.99 | Format: TP

Grant Morrison returns to the Man of Steel, joined by sensational artist Rags Morales to bring you the story of the early days of Superman.

SUPERMAN VOL. 1: WHAT PRICE TOMORROW?

Writer: George Pérez | Artists: Jesús Merino & Nicola Scott
ISBN: 978-1-4012-3468-3 | Diamond Code: JUL120210 | Price: $22.99 | Format: HC

The Man of Steel flies into the new DC Universe with a new status quo but a continued quest for truth and justice!

SUPERMAN: EARTH ONE VOL. 1

Writer: J. Michael Straczynski | Artist: Shane Davis
ISBN: 978-1-4012-2469-1 | Diamond Code: FEB130226 | Price: $12.99 | Format: TP

The #1 *New York Times* best–selling original graphic novel that re-imagines Superman as a brooding, reluctant hero in modern day Metropolis.

SUPERMAN: EARTH ONE VOL. 2

Writer: J. Michael Straczynski | Artist: Shane Davis
ISBN: 978-1-4012-3196-5 | Diamond Code: JUN120225 | Price: $22.99 | Format: HC

The sequel to the #1 *New York Times* best–selling original graphic novel by J. Michael Straczynski and Shane Davis.

SUPERMAN: BIRTHRIGHT

Writer: Mark Waid | Artist: Leinil Francis Yu
ISBN: 978-1-4012-0252-1 | Diamond Code: JUL050214 | Price: $19.99 | Format: TP

Superstar writer Mark Waid updates the origin of the Man of Steel in this classic tale.

ALL-STAR SUPERMAN

Writer: Grant Morrison | Artist: Frank Quitely
ISBN: 978-1-4012-3205-4 | Diamond Code: JUL110247 | Price: $29.99 | Format: TP

The critically acclaimed series that harkens back to the Golden Age of Superman by superstar writer Grant Morrison and artist Frank Quitely.

SUPERMAN: RED SON

Writer: Mark Millar | Artists: Dave Johnson & Kilian Plunkett
ISBN: 978-1-4012-0191-3 | Diamond Code: NOV058130 | Price: $17.99 | Format: TP

What if Superman's rocket crash landed in Russia? The Man of Steel is reimagined here as a Soviet hero.

GREEN LANTERN

When a dying alien crashes on Earth, reckless test pilot Hal Jordan is chosen to be that alien's successor in the Green Lantern Corps, a universe-wide peacekeeping force. The newest Green Lantern now faces his greatest fears and the most dangerous villains in the universe, armed with a power ring that has the ability to create anything he can imagine. Hal Jordan has become one of the most iconic and popular superheroes of DC Comics.

GREEN LANTERN: REBIRTH

Writer: Geoff Johns | Artist: Ethan Van Sciver
ISBN: 978-1-4012-2755-5 | Diamond Code: FEB100185 | Price: $14.99 | Format: TP

A jaw-dropping epic that reintroduces the quintessential Green Lantern, Hal Jordan!

GREEN LANTERN: NO FEAR

Writer: Geoff Johns | Artists: Carlos Pacheco & Ethan Van Sciver
ISBN: 978-1-4012-1058-8 | Diamond Code: FEB080244 | Price: $12.99 | Format: TP

Hal Jordan is back from the dead and tries to re-establish his life, though Manhunters and other villains stand in his way.

GREEN LANTERN: REVENGE OF THE GREEN LANTERNS

Writer: Geoff Johns | Artists: Carlos Pacheco & Ethan Van Sciver
ISBN: 978-1-4012-0960-5 | Diamond Code: JUN098401 | Price: $14.99 | Format: TP

Hal Jordan discovers that several long-lost Green Lanterns are still alive … and it's up to him to set them free.

GREEN LANTERN: WANTED: HAL JORDAN

Writer: Geoff Johns | Artists: Ivan Reis & Daniel Acuna
ISBN: 978-1-4012-1590-3 | Diamond Code: OCT080170 | Price: $14.99 | Format: TP

Hunted by the Global Guardians for a crime he didn't commit, can Hal clear his name before it's too late?

GREEN LANTERN: THE SINESTRO CORPS WAR

Writers: Geoff Johns, Dave Gibbons & Peter J. Tomasi
Artists: Ethan Van Sciver, Ivan Reis & Patrick Gleason
ISBN: 978-1-4012-3301-3 | Diamond Code: JUN110275 | Price: $29.99 | Format: TP

Sinestro—Hal Jordan's former mentor and archnemesis—has gathered an army of soldiers fueled by the fear to do war with the Green Lantern Corps.

GREEN LANTERN: SECRET ORIGIN

Writer: Geoff Johns | Artist: Ivan Reis
ISBN: 978-1-4012-2017-4 | Diamond Code: JAN110337 | Price: $14.99 | Format: TP

Witness the beginnings of the greatest Green Lantern of all in this title.

GREEN LANTERN: RAGE OF THE RED LANTERNS

Writer: Geoff Johns | Artists: Ivan Reis, Mike McKone & Shane Davis
ISBN: 978-1-4012-2302-1 | Diamond Code: APR100214 | Price: $14.99 | Format: TP

Hal Jordan battles for his life when the Red Lantern Corps, a brutal brigade of monsters fueled by rage, attacks!

GREEN LANTERN: AGENT ORANGE

Writer: Geoff Johns | Artist: Philip Tan
ISBN: 978-1-4012-2420-2 | Diamond Code: AUG100204 | Price: $14.99 | Format: TP

Hal Jordan must battle the bizarre Orange Lantern Corps and its leader, Agent Orange, as they threaten to consume the universe.

BLACKEST NIGHT

Writer: Geoff Johns | Artist: Ivan Reis
ISBN: 978-1-4012-2953-5 | Diamond Code: APR110192 | Price: $19.99 | Format: TP

Hal Jordan and the Green Lantern Corps lead DC's champions into battle to save the universe from an army of undead Black Lanterns!

BLACKEST NIGHT: GREEN LANTERN

Writer: Geoff Johns | Artist: Doug Mahnke
ISBN: 978-1-4012-2952-8 | Diamond Code: APR110193 | Price: $19.99 | Format: TP

The must-read companion graphic novel to the epic *Blackest Night*.

GREEN LANTERN: BRIGHTEST DAY

Writer: Geoff Johns | Artist: Doug Mahnke
ISBN: 978-1-4012-3141-5 | Diamond Code: FEB120254 | Price: $19.99 | Format: TP

The multi-colored Lantern Corps reluctantly team together to discover what (or who) is behind the mysterious White Lantern.

GREEN LANTERN: WAR OF THE GREEN LANTERNS

Writers: Geoff Johns, Tony Bedard & Peter J. Tomasi
Artists: Doug Mahnke, Tyler Kirkham & Fernando Pasarin
ISBN: 978-1-4012-3452-2 | Diamond Code: JUN120246 | Price: $16.99 | Format: TP

An ancient evil returns to destroy the Green Lanterns from within, as Corps-men turn on each other!

GREEN LANTERN VOL. 1: SINESTRO

Writer: Geoff Johns | Artist: Doug Mahnke
ISBN: 978-1-4012-3455-3 | Diamond Code: OCT120257 | Price: $14.99 | Format: TP

The red-hot team of writer Geoff Johns and Doug Mahnke light up the comic skies with the ring-slinging Corps and their newest member: Sinestro!

GREEN LANTERN CORPS: RECHARGE

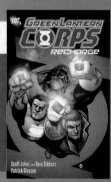

Writers: Geoff Johns & Dave Gibbons | Artist: Patrick Gleason
ISBN: 978-1-4012-0962-9 | Diamond Code: AUG098004 | Price: $14.99 | Format: TP
With the Guardians of the Universe returned, it is time to rebuild the fabled Green Lantern Corps!

GREEN LANTERN CORPS: TO BE A LANTERN

Writer: Dave Gibbons | Artist: Patrick Gleason
ISBN: 978-1-4012-1356-5 | Diamond Code: AUG098053 | Price: $14.99 | Format: TP

Comic book legend Dave Gibbons re-establishes the legendary Green Lantern Corps in this collection.

The FLASH

Young Barry Allen's life stopped the minute his mother was murdered and the mystery drove him to become a forensic scientist. When a freak lightning bolt hits a nearby shelf of chemicals in his lab, Barry receives super-speed, becoming THE FASTEST MAN ALIVE—THE FLASH!

THE FLASH: REBIRTH

Writer: Geoff Johns | Artist: Ethan Van Sciver
ISBN: 978-1-4012-3001-2 | Diamond Code: JAN110329 | Price: $14.99 | Format: TP

The explosive epic that reintroduces the newly returned Barry Allen as The Flash!

THE FLASH VOL. 1: THE DASTARDLY DEATH OF THE ROGUES!

Writer: Geoff Johns | Artist: Francis Manapul
ISBN: 978-1-4012-3195-8 | Diamond Code: OCT110249 | Price: $14.99 | Format: TP

The Fastest Man Alive must solve the murder of one of his greatest villains and protect his other foes from an elusive killer.

THE FLASH VOL. 2: THE ROAD TO FLASHPOINT

Writer: Geoff Johns | Artist: Francis Manapul
ISBN: 978-1-4012-3448-5 | Diamond Code: JUN120245 | Price: $14.99 | Format: TP

Make way for Hot Pursuit—the latest speedster to come out of the Speed Force in this super-charged story that ties directly into Flashpoint!

FLASHPOINT

Writer: Geoff Johns | Artist: Andy Kubert
ISBN: 978-1-4012-3338-9 | Diamond Code: DEC110276 | Price: $14.99 | Format: TP

Heroes become villains in an alternate universe tale that changed the DC Universe forever!

THE FLASH VOL. 1: MOVE FORWARD

Writers: Francis Manapul & Brian Buccellato | Artist: Francis Manapul
ISBN: 978-1-4012-3553-6 | Diamond Code: JUL120209 | Price: $24.99 | Format: HC

The Fastest Man Alive returns as Central City's greatest protector.

Oliver Queen had it all—movie star good looks, a matching cadre of women and his own billion dollar company. However, when the playboy became marooned on a desert island, he mastered the use of a bow and arrow to survive. Ollie eventually found his way back to his hometown, but with his priorities changed. Brandishing a new focus on bringing criminals to justice, he became the hero known as Green Arrow!

GREEN ARROW: YEAR ONE

Writer: Andy Diggle | Artist: Jock
ISBN: 978-14012-1743-3 | Diamond Code: JAN090227 | Price: $14.99 | Format: TP

Oliver's first year donning the quiver as Green Arrow!

GREEN LANTERN/GREEN ARROW

Writer: Denny O'Neil | Artist: Neal Adams
ISBN: 978-14012-3517-8 | Diamond Code: MAY120290 | Price: $29.99 | Format: TP

Classic team-ups between Green Arrow and Green Lantern, illustrated by legendary artist Neal Adams.

GREEN ARROW: THE LONGBOW HUNTERS

Writer: Mike Grell | Artist: Mike Grell
ISBN: 978-1-4012-3862-9 | Diamond Code: JUN120250 | Price: $14.99 | Format: TP

A gritty take on a vigilante Emerald Archer in this essential Green Arrow story by Mike Grell.

FOR MATURE READERS

GREEN ARROW: THE ARCHER'S QUEST

Writer: Brad Meltzer | Artist: Phil Hester
ISBN: 978-1-4012-0044-2 | Diamond Code: JUN120251 | Price: $14.99 | Format: TP

Oliver Queen returns to discover secrets from his past, in this graphic novel by *New York Times* best-selling novelist Brad Meltzer

GREEN ARROW VOL. 1: THE MIDAS TOUCH

Writer: J.T. Krul & Keith Giffen | Artists: Dan Jurgens & George Pérez
ISBN: 978-1-4012-3486-7 | Diamond Code: FEB120249 | Price: $14.99 | Format: TP

Re-imagines the sharp-shooting, emerald-clad DC hero Oliver Queen, also known as Green Arrow!

The World's Greatest Super Heroes: Superman, Batman, Wonder Woman, Green Lantern, The Flash, Aquaman, and Cyborg. Greater than the sum of their awe-inspiring parts, the Justice League handles threats too massive for any single hero.

JLA VOL. 1

Writer: Grant Morrison | Artists: Howard Porter & Oscar Jimenez
ISBN: 978-1-4012-3314-3 | Diamond Code: JUN110276 | Price: $19.99 | Format: TP

Grant Morrison relaunches the greatest team in the DC Universe—returning the powerhouse lineup of Superman, Batman, Wonder Woman, The Flash, Green Lantern, Aquaman and Martian Manhunter!

JLA: EARTH 2

Writer: Grant Morrison | Artist: Frank Quitely
ISBN: 978-1-4012-4095-0 | Diamond Code: AUG120253 | Price: $14.99 | Format: TP

The Justice League battle their Earth 2 counterparts: the evil Crime Syndicate of Amerika!

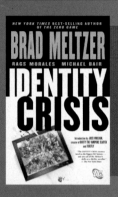

IDENTITY CRISIS

Writer: Brad Meltzer | Artist: Rags Morales
ISBN: 978-1-4012-0458-7 | Diamond Code: AUG118125 | Price: $17.99 | Format: TP

Uncover the DC Universe's deadliest secret in this acclaimed miniseries from *New York Times* best-selling novelist Brad Meltzer.

JUSTICE LEAGUE OF AMERICA VOL. 1: THE TORNADO'S PATH

Writer: Brad Meltzer | Artist: Ed Benes
ISBN: 978-1-4012-1580-4 | Diamond Code: JUN080244 | Price: $17.99 | Format: TP

The *New York Times* best-selling author Brad Meltzer redefines the World's Greatest Super Team for a new generation.

JUSTICE LEAGUE OF AMERICA VOL. 2: THE LIGHTNING SAGA

Writers: Brad Meltzer & Geoff Johns
Artists: Ed Benes, Shane Davis, Fernando Pasarin, Gene Ha & Dale Eaglesham
ISBN: 978-1-4012-1869-0 | Diamond Code: OCT080173 | Price: $17.99 | Format: TP

The Justice League teams with the Justice Society and the Legion of Super-Heroes to unravel a mystery plaguing all three teams.

JUSTICE LEAGUE VOL 1: ORIGIN

Writer: Geoff Johns | Artist: Jim Lee
ISBN: 978-1-4012-3788-2 | Diamond Code: OCT120252 | Price: $16.99 | Format: TP

Geoff Johns and Jim Lee unite for the first time to launch the bold beginning of the DC Universe's premier super team!

DC: THE NEW FRONTIER VOL. 1

Writer: Darwyn Cooke | Artist: Darwyn Cooke
ISBN: 978-1-4012-0350-4 | Diamond Code: FEB058027 | Price: $19.99 | Format: TP

Darwyn Cooke's acclaimed journey from the end of the Golden Age to the genesis of a bold new heroic era in the late 1950s!

JUSTICE LEAGUE OF AMERICA: THE NAIL

Writer: Alan Davis | Artist: Alan Davis
ISBN: 978-1-5638-9480-0 | Diamond Code: MAR045122 | Price: $14.95 | Format: TP

What if a simple nail prevented the Kents from discovering the rocket ship that day? What would a world without Superman look like?

JUSTICE

Writers: Alex Ross & Jim Krueger | Artists: Alex Ross & Doug Braithwaite
ISBN: 978-1-4012-3526-0 | Diamond Code: MAR120254 | Price: $29.99 | Format: TP

The world's deadliest super villains band together to ... save the world? The Justice League must discover what's at the bottom of this mystery in Alex Ross's superb graphic novel.

KINGDOM COME

Writer: Mark Waid | Artist: Alex Ross
ISBN: 978-1-4012-2034-1 | Diamond Code: JUN080246 | Price: $17.99 | Format: TP

The unforgettable, best-selling miniseries from acclaimed writer Mark Waid and superstar painter Alex Ross that pits new and old eras of heroes against each other.

Women of DC Comics

Batman, Superman, Green Lantern, and The Flash are some of the most recognized pop culture icons in the world. But not to be outdone by their male counterparts, the Women of the DC Universe are just as powerful, and in some cases, more dangerous. Wonder Woman, Catwoman, Batgirl, and Batwoman soar in their own tales and series in some of DC Comics' greatest stories ever told.

WONDER WOMAN: ODYSSEY VOL. 1

Writers: J. Michael Straczynski & Phil Hester | Artists: Don Kramer, Eduardo Pansica & others
ISBN: 978-1-4012-3078-4 | Diamond Code: APR120258 | Price: $14.99 | Format: TP

If you think you knew who Wonder Woman was—think again! All bets are off in this all-new direction for the long-running series that's perfect for new readers!

WONDER WOMAN: ODYSSEY VOL. 2

Writers: J. Michael Straczynski & Phil Hester | Artists: Don Kramer, Eduardo Pansica & others
ISBN: 978-1-4012-3432-4 | Diamond Code: NOV120274 | Price: $16.99 | Format: TP

Diana, a.k.a. Wonder Woman, must track down the truth behind who or what destroyed Paradise Island.

WONDER WOMAN VOL. 1: BLOOD

Writer: Brian Azzarello | Artists: Cliff Chiang & Tony Akins
ISBN: 978-1-4012-3562-8 | Diamond Code: OCT120256 | Price: $14.99 | Format: TP

Superheroics and ancient myth meet, as critically acclaimed writer Brian Azzarello teams with Cliff Chiang and Tony Akins to begin a new chapter for the Amazon Princess.

BATGIRL VOL. 1: THE DARKEST REFLECTION

Writer: Gail Simone | Artist: Ardian Syaf
ISBN: 978-1-4012-3814-8 | Diamond Code: NOV120261 | Price: $14.99 | Format: TP

Barbara Gordon is back as Batgirl—and she's going to have to face the city's most horrifying new villains as well as the dark secrets from her past.

BATWOMAN: ELEGY

Writer: Greg Rucka | Artist: J.H. Williams III
ISBN: 978-1-4012-3146-0 | Diamond Code: MAR110341 | Price: $17.99 | Format: TP

Batwoman is re-introduced for a new generation of readers, as Gotham City's newest protector battles a madwoman that threatens her past as well as her present!

BATWOMAN VOL. 1: HYDROLOGY

Writers: J.H. Williams III & W. Haden Blackman | Artist: J.H. Williams III
ISBN: 978-1-4012-3784-4 | Diamond Code: OCT120253 | Price: $14.99 | Format: TP

The Batwoman Kate Kane defends the streets of Gotham City in her very own self-titled series!

CATWOMAN: WHEN IN ROME

Writer: Jeph Loeb | Artist: Tim Sale
ISBN: 978-1-4012-0717-5 | Diamond Code: MAY098043 | Price: $14.99 | Format: TP

In this sequel to the events of *Batman: The Long Halloween* and *Batman: Dark Victory*, Catwoman learns about her dark past in Rome.

CATWOMAN VOL. 1: THE GAME

Writer: Judd Winick | Artist: Guillem March
ISBN: 978-1-4012-3464-5 | Diamond Code: FEB120248 | Price: $14.99 | Format: TP

Addicted to danger, what happens when Catwoman steals from the wrong man? Writer Judd Winick begins a new chapter for Selina Kyle!

HUNTRESS: CROSSBOW AT THE CROSSROADS

Writer: Paul Levitz | Artist: Marcus To
ISBN: 978-1-4012-3733-2 | Diamond Code: JUL120223 | Price: $14.99 | Format: TP

Huntress creator Paul Levitz returns in this action-packed journey through the bowels of Italy's most deadly crime syndicates.

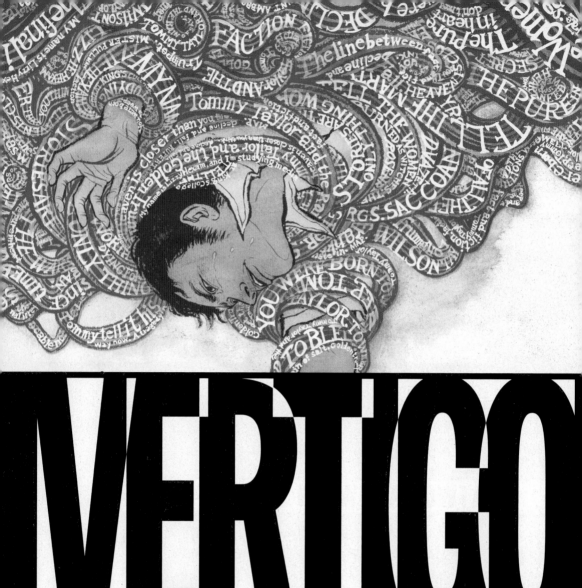

VERTIGO

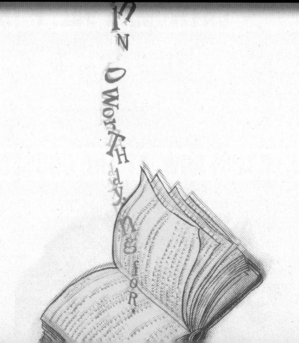

TOP SERIES

FOR MATURE READERS

100 BULLETS VOL. 1: FIRST SHOT, LAST CALL

Writer: Brian Azzarello | Artist: Eduardo Risso
ISBN: 978-1-5638-9645-3 | Diamond Code: JAN128095 | Price: $12.99 | Format: TP

Guaranteed full immunity, what would you do? Vertigo's seminal crime series features ordinary citizens who are given the opportunity to exact revenge on a person who has wronged them.

AMERICAN VAMPIRE VOL. 1

Writers: Scott Snyder & Stephen King | Artist: Rafael Albuquerque
ISBN: 978-1-4012-2974-0 | Diamond Code: JUL110284 | Price: $19.99 | Format: TP

Scott Snyder and Stephen King set fire to the horror genre with a visionary take on one of pop culture's most infamous monsters, as they trace the creatures' bloodline through decades of American history.

DAYTRIPPER

Writer: Gabriel Bá | Artist: Fábio Moon
ISBN: 978-1-4012-2969-6 | Diamond Code: NOV100268 | Price: $19.99 | Format: TP

This award-winning graphic novel follows Bras de Olivias Dominguez during different periods in his life, each with the same ending: his death.

DMZ VOL. 1: ON THE GROUND

Writer: Brian Wood | Artist: Riccardo Burchielli
ISBN: 978-1-4012-1062-5 | Diamond Code: OCT118125 | Price: $12.99 | Format: TP

In the near future after a second American Civil War, Manhattan becomes a wasteland known as the DMZ. Matty Roth, a naïve aspiring photojournalist, must cover the war zone from the inside … if he can survive.

EX MACHINA VOL. 1: THE FIRST HUNDRED DAYS

Writer: Brian K. Vaughan | Artist: Tony Harris
ISBN: 978-1-4012-0612-3 | Diamond Code: SEP108201 | Price: $12.99 | Format: TP

Tired of risking his life day-in and day-out, superhero Mitchell Hundred becomes the Mayor of New York City in this thrilling graphic novel from the creator of Y: The Last Man.

THE GIRL WITH THE DRAGON TATTOO BOOK 1

Writer: Denise Mina | Artists: Leonardo Manco & Andrea Mutti
ISBN: 978-1-4012-3557-4 | Diamond Code: JUL120243 | Price: $19.99 | Format: HC

A graphic novel adaptation of the #1 international bestseller and box office smash hit.

iZOMBIE VOL. 1: DEAD TO THE WORLD

Writer: Chris Roberson | Artist: Mike Allred
ISBN: 978-1-4012-2965-8 | Diamond Code: DEC100299 | Price: $14.99 | Format: TP

The everyday stories of twenty-something zombie Gwen Dylan, as she makes her way along in this living world.

JOHN CONSTANTINE, HELLBLAZER: ORIGINAL SINS

Writer: Jamie Delano | Artists: John Ridgway, Alfredo Alcala & Rick Veitch
ISBN: 978-1-4012-3006-7 | Diamond Code: DEC100302 | Price: $19.99 | Format: TP

Vertigo's longest running series featuring the antihero, John Constantine, England's chain-smoking, low-rent magician.

THE LOSERS BOOK ONE

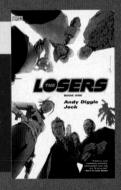

Writer: Andy Diggle | Artist: Jock
ISBN: 978-1-4012-2733-3 | Diamond Code: NOV090232 | Price: $19.99 | Format: TP

A team of former elite U.S. Special Forces soldiers, the Losers, hunt down the government forces that betrayed them.

NORTHLANDERS VOL. 1: SVEN THE RETURNED

Writer: Brian Wood | Artist: Davide Gianfelice
ISBN: 978-1-4012-1918-5 | Diamond Code: AUG118083 | Price: $16.99 | Format: TP

Fresh, violent, contemporary takes on ancient viking warrior adventures.

PREACHER VOL. 1: GONE TO TEXAS

Writer: Garth Ennis | Artist: Steve Dillon
ISBN: 978-1-5638-9261-5 | Diamond Code: JUL108037 | Price: $17.99 | Format: TP

Jesse Custer, a wayward preacher, begins a violent journey to find God (literally), joined by his girlfriend Tulip and the hard-drinking Irish vampire Cassidy.

SCALPED VOL. 1: INDIAN COUNTRY

Writer: Jason Aaron | Artist: R.M. Guera
ISBN: 978-1-4012-1317-6 | Diamond Code: APR108251 | Price: $14.99 | Format: TP

Dashiell Bad Horse must return to the reservation he grew up in, determined to clean up the crime-ridden "Rez" he left years ago, one way or another.

SWEET TOOTH VOL. 1: OUT OF THE DEEP WOODS

Writer: Jeff Lemire | Artist: Jeff Lemire
ISBN: 978-1-4012-2696-1 | Diamond Code: AUG108007 | Price: $12.99 | Format: TP

Gus—a boy born with deer-like antlers—is left to survive in an American landscape devastated a decade earlier by an inexplicable pandemic.

TRANSMETROPOLITAN VOL. 1: BACK ON THE STREET

Writer: Warren Ellis | Artist: Darick Robertson
ISBN: 978-1-4012-2084-6 | Diamond Code: DEC080220 | Price: $14.99 | Format: TP

Mastermind writer Warren Ellis delivers this sharp, manic, anything-goes exploration of urban life about journalist/cult author Spider Jerusalem.

THE UNWRITTEN VOL. 1: TOMMY TAYLOR AND THE BOGUS IDENTITY

Writer: Mike Carey | Artist: Peter Gross
ISBN: 978-1-4012-2565-0 | Diamond Code: APR128238 | Price: $14.99 | Format: TP

Tom Taylor, the inspiration for the boy wizard from the series of novels his father made famous, finds that the worlds of fiction and real life are crossing over into each other in this fantastic graphic novel.

One of the most popular and critically acclaimed graphic novels of all time, Neil Gaiman's award-winning masterpiece THE SANDMAN has set the standard for mature, lyrical fantasy in the comic book field. Illustrated by a rotating cast of the medium's most sought-after artists, the series is a rich blend of modern and ancient mythology into which contemporary fiction, historical drama and legend are seamlessly interwoven.

NEIL GAIMAN'S
SANDMAN

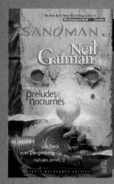

THE SANDMAN VOL. 1: PRELUDES & NOCTURNES

Writer: Neil Gaiman | Artists: Mike Dringenberg, Sam Kieth & Malcolm Jones III
ISBN: 978-1-4012-2575-9 | Diamond Code: JUL100259 | Price: $19.99 | Format: TP

Collects issues #1-8.

THE SANDMAN VOL. 2: THE DOLL'S HOUSE

Writer: Neil Gaiman
Artists: Mike Dringenberg, Sam Kieth, Malcolm Jones III, Chris Bachalo & Michael Zulli
ISBN: 978-1-4012-2799-9 | Diamond Code: JUL100260 | Price: $19.99 | Format: TP

Collects issues #9-16.

THE SANDMAN VOL. 3: DREAM COUNTRY

Writer: Neil Gaiman
Artists: Mike Dringenberg, Kelley Jones, Malcolm Jones III, Colleen Doran & Charles Vess
ISBN: 978-1-4012-2935-1 | Diamond Code: JUL100261 | Price: $19.99 | Format: TP

Collects issues #17-20.

THE SANDMAN VOL. 4: SEASON OF MISTS

Writer: Neil Gaiman
Artists: Kelley Jones, Malcolm Jones III, P. Craig Russell & Matt Wagner
ISBN: 978-1-4012-3042-5 | Diamond Code: OCT100330 | Price: $19.99 | Format: TP

Collects issues #21-28.

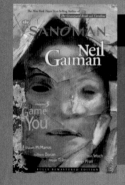

THE SANDMAN VOL. 5: A GAME OF YOU

Writer: Neil Gaiman
Artists: Shawn McManus, Colleen Doran, Stan Woch, Bryan Talbot & others
ISBN: 978-1-4012-3043-2 | Diamond Code: JAN110431 | Price: $19.99 | Format: TP

Collects issues #32-37.

THE SANDMAN VOL. 6: FABLES & REFLECTIONS

Writer: Neil Gaiman
Artists: Shawn McManus, P. Craig Russell, Stan Woch, Bryan Talbot, Jill Thompson & others
ISBN: 978-1-4012-3123-1 | Diamond Code: MAY110297 | Price: $19.99 | Format: TP

Collects issues #29-31, #38-40 and #50.

THE SANDMAN VOL. 7: BRIEF LIVES

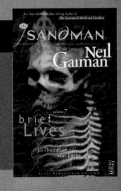

Writer: Neil Gaiman | Artist: Jill Thompson & Vince Locke
ISBN: 978-1-4012-3263-4 | Diamond Code: SEP110177 | Price: $19.99 | Format: TP

Collects issues #41-49.

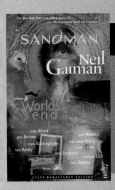

THE SANDMAN VOL. 8: WORLDS' END

Writer: Neil Gaiman
Artists: Mike Allred, Mark Buckingham, Michael Zulli, Tony Harris & others
ISBN: 978-1-4012-3402-7 | Diamond Code: NOV110233 | Price: $19.99 | Format: TP

Collects issues #51-56.

THE SANDMAN VOL. 9: THE KINDLY ONES

Writer: Neil Gaiman
Artists: Marc Hempel, Richard Case, Charles Vess, Kevin Nowlan & others
ISBN: 978-1-4012-3545-1 | Diamond Code: FEB120298 | Price: $19.99 | Format: TP

Collects issues #57-69 and *Vertigo Jam* #1.

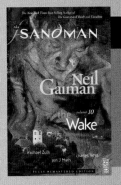

THE SANDMAN VOL. 10: THE WAKE

Writer: Neil Gaiman | Artists: Michael Zulli, Charles Vess & Jon J Muth
ISBN: 978-1-4012-3754-7 | Diamond Code: AUG120292 | Price: $19.99 | Format: TP

Collects issues #70-75.

THE SANDMAN: ENDLESS NIGHTS

Writer: Neil Gaiman

Artists: Frank Quitely, Glenn Fabry, Bill Sienkiewicz, P. Craig Russell & others

ISBN: 978-1-4012-0113-5 | Diamond Code: DEC068187 | Price: $19.99 | Format: TP

Seven stories featuring the Sandman and his siblings, the Endless, with art from the industry's finest illustrators.

THE SANDMAN: THE DREAM HUNTERS

Writer: Neil Gaiman | Artist: Yoshitaka Amano

ISBN: 978-1-5638-9629-3 | Diamond Code: DEC068030 | Price: $19.99 | Format: TP

A novella with stunning art from Japanese artist Yoshitaka Amano.

THE SANDMAN: THE DREAM HUNTERS

Writer: Neil Gaiman | Artist: P. Craig Russell

ISBN: 978-1-4912-2428-8 | Diamond Code: JUN100280 | Price: $19.99 | Format: TP

P. Craig Russell's traditional comic book adaptation of the breakthrough original graphic novel.

DEATH: THE HIGH COST OF LIVING

Writer: Neil Gaiman | Artists: Chris Bachalo & Mark Buckingham

ISBN: 978-1-4012-2428-8 | Diamond Code: JUL058228 | Price: $12.99 | Format: TP

Every 100 years, Death takes on human form to learn the cost—and value— of life in this landmark series.

DEATH: THE DELUXE EDITION

Writer: Neil Gaiman | Artists: Chris Bachalo & Mark Buckingham

ISBN: 978-1-4012-3548-2 | Diamond Code: JUN120272 | Price: $29.99 | Format: HC

Vertigo's Death stories are all captured here in one, over-sized deluxe edition graphic novel.

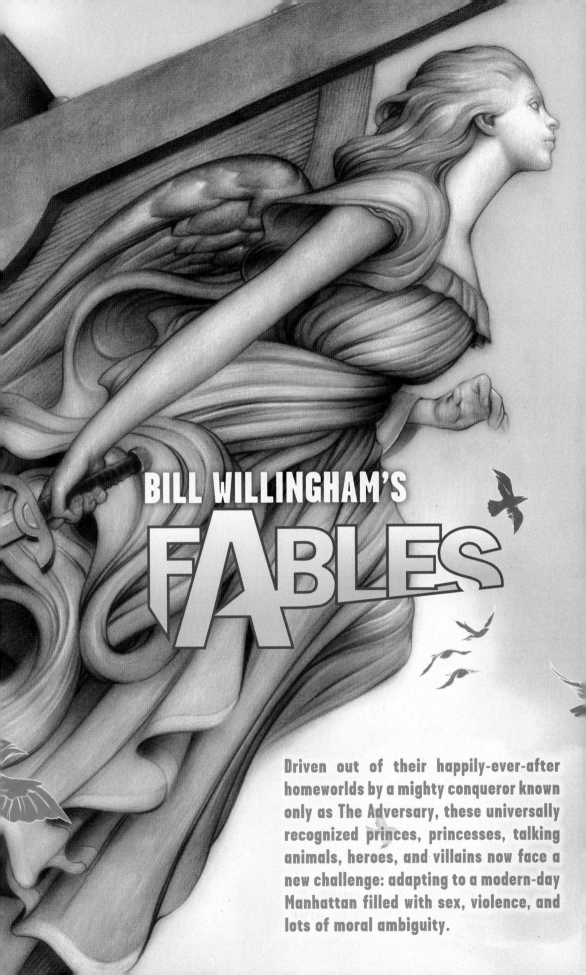

BILL WILLINGHAM'S
FABLES

Driven out of their happily-ever-after homeworlds by a mighty conqueror known only as The Adversary, these universally recognized princes, princesses, talking animals, heroes, and villains now face a new challenge: adapting to a modern-day Manhattan filled with sex, violence, and lots of moral ambiguity.

FABLES VOL. 1: LEGENDS IN EXILE

Writer: Bill Willingham | Artist: Lan Medina
ISBN: 978-1-4012-3755-4 | Diamond Code: FEB120285 | Price: $12.99 | Format: TP

Collects issues #1-5.

FABLES VOL. 2: ANIMAL FARM

Writer: Bill Willingham | Artist: Mark Buckingham
ISBN: 978-1-4012-0077-0 | Diamond Code: MAR058123 | Price: $12.99 | Format: TP

Collects issues #6-10.

FABLES VOL. 3: STORYBOOK LOVE

Writer: Bill Willingham | Artist: Mark Buckingham
ISBN: 978-1-4012-0256-9 | Diamond Code: JAN128247 | Price: $16.99 | Format: TP

Collects issues #11-18.

FABLES VOL. 4: MARCH OF THE WOODEN SOLDIERS

Writer: Bill Willingham | Artist: Mark Buckingham
ISBN: 978-1-4012-0222-4 | Diamond Code: OCT058021 | Price: $17.99 | Format: TP

Collects issues #19-21 and #23-27.

FABLES VOL. 5: THE MEAN SEASONS

Writer: Bill Willingham | Artist: Mark Buckingham
ISBN: 978-1-4012-0486-0 | Diamond Code: JAN050373 | Price: $14.99 | Format: TP

Collects issues #22 and #28-33.

FABLES VOL. 6: HOMELANDS

Writer: Bill Willingham | Artist: Mark Buckingham
ISBN: 978-1-4012-0500-3 | Diamond Code: OCT050317 | Price: $14.99 | Format: TP

Collects issues #34-41.

FABLES VOL. 7: ARABIAN NIGHTS (AND DAYS)

Writer: Bill Willingham | Artist: Mark Buckingham
ISBN: 978-1-4012-1000-7 | Diamond Code: MAR060384 | Price: $14.99 | Format: TP

Collects issues #42-47.

FABLES VOL. 8: WOLVES

Writer: Bill Willingham | Artist: Mark Buckingham
ISBN: 978-1-4012-1001-4 | Diamond Code: SEP060313 | Price: $17.99 | Format: TP

Collects issues #48-51.

FABLES VOL. 9: SONS OF EMPIRE

Writer: Bill Willingham | Artist: Mark Buckingham
ISBN: 978-1-4012-1316-9 | Diamond Code: MAR070271 | Price: $17.99 | Format: TP

Collects issues #52-59.

FABLES VOL. 10: THE GOOD PRINCE

Writer: Bill Willingham | Artist: Mark Buckingham
ISBN: 978-1-4012-1686-3 | Diamond Code: FEB080297 | Price: $17.99 | Format: TP

Collects issues #60-69.

FABLES VOL. 11: WAR AND PIECES

Writer: Bill Willingham | Artist: Mark Buckingham
ISBN: 978-1-4012-1913-0 | Diamond Code: AUG080229 | Price: $17.99 | Format: TP

Collects issues #70-75.

FABLES VOL. 12: THE DARK AGES

Writer: Bill Willingham | Artist: Mark Buckingham
ISBN: 978-1-4012-2316-8 | Diamond Code: MAY090236 | Price: $17.99 | Format: TP

Collects issues #76-82.

FABLES VOL. 13: THE GREAT FABLES CROSSOVER

Writers: Bill Willingham & Matt Sturges | Artists: Mark Buckingham & Tony Akins
ISBN: 978-1-4012-2572-8 | Diamond Code: NOV090228 | Price: $17.99 | Format: TP

Collects issues #83-85, *Jack of Fables* #33-35 and *The Literals* #1-3.

FABLES VOL. 14: WITCHES

Writer: Bill Willingham | Artist: Mark Buckingham
ISBN: 978-1-4012-2880-4 | Diamond Code: SEP100304 | Price: $17.99 | Format: TP

Collects issues #86-93.

FABLES VOL. 15: ROSE RED

Writer: Bill Willingham | Artist: Mark Buckingham
ISBN: 978-1-4012-3000-5 | Diamond Code: JAN110422 | Price: $17.99 | Format: TP

Collects issues #94-100.

FABLES VOL. 16: SUPER TEAM

Writer: Bill Willingham | Artist: Mark Buckingham
ISBN: 978-1-4012-3306-8 | Diamond Code: SEP110221 | Price: $14.99 | Format: TP

Collects issues #101-107.

FABLES VOL. 17: INHERIT THE WIND

Writer: Bill Willingham | Artist: Mark Buckingham
ISBN: 978-1-4012-3516-1 | Diamond Code: APR120282 | Price: $14.99 | Format: TP

Collects issues #108-113.

PETER & MAX: A FABLES NOVEL

Writer: Bill Willingham | Illustrations: Steve Leialoha
ISBN: 978-1-4012-2537-7 | Diamond Code: SEP100303 | Price: $14.99 | Format: TP

In this original prose novel, two brothers must survive in the deepest dark of the Black Forest.

FABLES: 1001 NIGHTS OF SNOWFALL

Writer: Bill Willingham

Artists: Brian Bolland, Charles Vess, Jill Thompson, Mark Buckingham & others

ISBN: 978-1-4012-0369-6 | Diamond Code: DEC070297 | Price: $14.99 | Format: TP

Snow White charms a young sultan with untold tales of the citizens of Fabletown in this graphic novel anthology.

FABLES: WEREWOLVES OF THE HEARTLAND

Writer: Bill Willingham | Artists: Jim Fern & Craig Hamilton

ISBN: 978-1-4012-2479-0 | Diamond Code: JUL120247 | Price: $22.99 | Format: HC

Bigby Wolf travels across America on a quest for a new settlement for his fellow Fables, but finds himself caught in a small town of werewolves.

FAIREST VOL. 1: WIDE AWAKE

Writer: Bill Willingham | Artist: Phil Jimenez

ISBN: 978-1-4012-3550-5 | Diamond Code: AUG120283 | Price: $14.99 | Format: TP

The lovely and dangerous women of Fabletown get their own series.

JACK OF FABLES VOL. 1: THE (NEARLY) GREAT ESCAPE

Writers: Bill Willingham & Matt Sturges | Artist: Tony Akins

ISBN: 978-1-4012-1222-3 | Diamond Code: NOV060300 | Price: $14.99 | Format: TP

The irascible con man Jack Horner takes Hollywood by storm in this *Fables* spin-off.

CINDERELLA: FROM FABLETOWN WITH LOVE

Writer: Chris Roberson | Artist: Shawn McManus

ISBN: 978-1-4012-2750-0 | Diamond Code: MAY100268 | Price: $14.99 | Format: TP

Cinderella—globe-trotting secret agent—embarks on a mission to find out who's secretly smuggling powerful magical artifacts out of Fabletown.

CINDERELLA: FABLES ARE FOREVER

Writer: Chris Roberson | Artist: Shawn McManus

ISBN: 978-1-4012-3385-3 | Diamond Code: JAN120331 | Price: $14.99 | Format: TP

A threat from Cinderella's black-ops past comes back to haunt her.

In 2002, every man, boy and mammal with a Y chromosome dies during a worldwide epidemic. Every man except for one. Yorick Brown and his monkey Ampersand are the only two males to survive and commence a years-long odyssey to discover why. Writer Brian K. Vaughan and artist Pia Guerra bring to vivid life the age-old speculation: What would really happen to the last man on Earth?

BRIAN K. VAUGHAN'S
THE LAST MAN

Y: THE LAST MAN VOL. 1: UNMANNED

Writer: Brian K. Vaughan | Artist: Pia Guerra
ISBN: 978-1-5638-9980-5 | Diamond Code: DEC108152 | Price: $14.99 | Format: TP

Collects issues #1-5.

Y: THE LAST MAN VOL. 2: CYCLES

Writer: Brian K. Vaughan | Artist: Pia Guerra
ISBN: 978-1-4012-0076-3 | Diamond Code: SEP128229 | Price: $14.99 | Format: TP

Collects issues #6-10.

Y: THE LAST MAN VOL. 3: ONE SMALL STEP

Writer: Brian K. Vaughan | Artist: Pia Guerra
ISBN: 978-1-4012-0201-9 | Diamond Code: FEB118093 | Price: $14.99 | Format: TP

Collects issues #11-17.

Y: THE LAST MAN VOL. 4: SAFEWORD

Writer: Brian K. Vaughan | Artist: Pia Guerra
ISBN: 978-1-4012-0232-3 | Diamond Code: DEC108199 | Price: $14.99 | Format: TP

Collects issues #18-23.

Y: THE LAST MAN VOL. 5: RING OF TRUTH

Writer: Brian K. Vaughan | Artist: Pia Guerra
ISBN: 978-1-4012-0487-7 | Diamond Code: MAY050306 | Price: $14.99 | Format: TP

Collects issues #24-31.

Y: THE LAST MAN VOL. 6: GIRL ON GIRL

Writer: Brian K. Vaughan | Artist: Pia Guerra
ISBN: 978-1-4012-0501-0 | Diamond Code: DEC108151 | Price: $14.99 | Format: TP

Collects issues #32-36.

Y: THE LAST MAN VOL. 7: PAPER DOLLS

Writer: Brian K. Vaughan | Artist: Pia Guerra
ISBN: 978-1-4012-1009-0 | Diamond Code: FEB060341 | Price: $14.99 | Format: TP

Collects issues #37-42.

Y: THE LAST MAN VOL. 8: KIMONO DRAGONS

Writer: Brian K. Vaughan | Artist: Pia Guerra
ISBN: 978-1-4012-1010-6 | Diamond Code: AUG060299 | Price: $14.99 | Format: TP

Collects issues #43-48.

Y: THE LAST MAN VOL. 9: MOTHERLAND

Writer: Brian K. Vaughan | Artist: Pia Guerra
ISBN: 978-1-4012-1351-0 | Diamond Code: FEB070362 | Price: $14.99 | Format: TP

Collects issues #49-54.

Y: THE LAST MAN VOL. 10: WHYS AND WHEREFORES

Writer: Brian K. Vaughan | Artist: Pia Guerra
ISBN: 978-1-4012-1813-3 | Diamond Code: MAR080241 | Price: $14.99 | Format: TP

Collects issues #55-60.

ALAN MOORE

ALAN MOORE has crafted some of the most celebrated and cherished stories the comic book industry has ever seen, breaking new ground with titles such as SAGA OF THE SWAMP THING and the best-selling graphic novel of all time, WATCHMEN. His work on titles such as THE LEAGUE OF EXTRAORDINARY GENTLEMEN, PROMETHEA and V FOR VENDETTA has defined a generation of readers and helped usher in an era in which the graphic novel became a serious form of artistic expression.

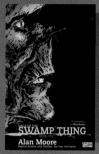

SAGA OF THE SWAMP THING BOOK ONE

Writer: Alan Moore | Artists: Stephen Bissette
ISBN: 978-1-4012-2083-9 | Diamond Code: JAN120343 | Price: $19.99 | Format: TP

Alan Moore's take on the classic monster that stretched the creative boundaries of the medium and became one of the most spectacular series in comic book history.

V FOR VENDETTA

Writer: Alan Moore | Artist: David Lloyd
ISBN: 978-1-4012-0841-7 | Diamond Code: SEP088030 | Price: $19.99 | Format: TP

Alan Moore's iconic tale set in a near-future dystopian London and its revolutionary hero "V."

PROMETHEA BOOK 1

Writer: Alan Moore | Artist: J.H. Williams III
ISBN: 978-1-5638-9667-5 | Diamond Code: APR108106 | Price: $17.99 | Format: TP

Alan Moore's psychedelic tale of Sophia, an ordinary college student who is transformed into Promethea, the living embodiment of imagination.

THE LEAGUE OF EXTRAORDINARY GENTLEMEN VOL. 1

Writer: Alan Moore | Artist: Kevin O'Neill
ISBN: 978-1-5638-9858-7 | Diamond Code: MAY118167 | Price: $16.99 | Format: TP

The best-known characters of 19th Century literature band together in Alan Moore's award-winning graphic novel.

THE LEAGUE OF EXTRAORDINARY GENTLEMEN VOL. 2

Writer: Alan Moore | Artist: Kevin O'Neill
ISBN: 978-1-4012-0118-0 | Diamond Code: MAY118168 | Price: $16.99 | Format: TP

The League must reassemble to combat an impending invasion.

THE LEAGUE OF EXTRAORDINARY GENTLEMEN: BLACK DOSSIER

Writer: Alan Moore | Artist: Kevin O'Neill
ISBN: 978-1-4012-0307-8 | Diamond Code: JUL080193 | Price: $19.99 | Format: TP

Disbanded and disavowed, the remaining members of the League search for the Black Dossier to save the country from an iron-fisted regime.

GRANT MORRISON has been working with Vertigo for twenty years, creating some of the most seminal works in the imprint's history, starting with ANIMAL MAN and DOOM PATROL. His reality-bending themes, provocative storytelling and otherwordly concepts have endeared him to mainstream culture at-large as one of the most groundbreaking minds in the medium.

GRANT MORRISON

ANIMAL MAN VOL. 1

Writer: Grant Morrison | Artists: Chas Truog, Doug Hazlewood & Tom Grummet
ISBN: 978-1-5638-9005-5 | Diamond Code: OCT068037 | Price: $19.99 | Format: TP

The bizarre adventures of Animal Man, a second-rate super-hero struggling with real-life issues and moral dilemmas.

DOOM PATROL VOL. 1: CRAWLING FROM THE WRECKAGE

Writer: Grant Morrison | Artists: Richard Case, Doug Braithwaite & others
ISBN: 978-1-5638-9034-5 | Diamond Code: JAN058100 | Price: $19.99 | Format: TP

Grant Morrison reinvents the strange superhero team.

FLEX MENTALLO: MAN OF MUSCLE MYSTERY

Writer: Grant Morrison | Artist: Frank Quitely
ISBN: 978-1-4012-3221-4 | Diamond Code: OCT110285 | Price: $22.99 | Format: HC

From the pages of *Doom Patrol*, the award-winning team behind *All-Star Superman* take on Flex Mentallo.

JOE THE BARBARIAN

Writer: Grant Morrison | Artist: Sean Murphy
ISBN: 978-1-4012-3747-9 | Diamond Code: DEC120365 | Price: $19.99 | Format: TP

Thirteen-year-old diabetic Joe Manson is transported to a fantasy land where he's the world's last hope.

THE INVISIBLES VOL. 1: SAY YOU WANT A REVOLUTION

Writer: Grant Morrison | Artists: Steve Yeowell & Jill Thompson
ISBN: 978-1-5638-9267-7 | Diamond Code: SEP068118 | Price: $19.99 | Format: TP

Throughout history, a secret society called the Invisibles has worked against dark forces conspiring to end mankind.

WE3

Writer: Grant Morrison | Artist: Frank Quitely
ISBN: 978-1-4012-3067-8 | Diamond Code: FEB110270 | Price: $24.99 | Format: HC

Grant Morrison and Frank Quitely deliver the emotional journey of three housepets who are weaponized for lethal combat by the government.

MAD

For fifty years, MAD has been a staple of bedrooms, living rooms, dorm rooms and recycling bins. Irreverent as ever, MAD continues to satirize and parody

THE MAD ARCHIVES VOL. 1

By: The Usual Gang Of Idiots
ISBN: 978-1-4012-3786-8 | Diamond Code: APR120274 | Price: $59.99 | Format: HC

Collects the original *MAD* series issues #1-6.

THE MAD ARCHIVES VOL. 2

By: The Usual Gang Of Idiots
ISBN: 978-1-4012-3787-5 | Diamond Code: APR120275 | Price: $59.99 | Format: HC

Collects the original *MAD* series issues #7-12.

THE MAD ARCHIVES VOL. 3

By: The Usual Gang Of Idiots
ISBN: 978-1-4012-3427-0 | Diamond Code: SEP110209 | Price: $59.99 | Format: HC

Collects the original *MAD* series issues #13-18.

THE MAD ARCHIVES VOL. 4

By: The Usual Gang Of Idiots
ISBN: 978-1-4012-3761-5 | Diamond Code: APR120273 | Price: $59.99 | Format: HC

Collects the original *MAD* series issues #19-24.

AMAZINGLY STUPID MAD

By: The Usual Gang Of Idiots
ISBN: 978-1-4012-3857-5 | Diamond Code: MAY120312 | Price: $12.99 | Format: TP

Ripped from the pages of *MAD Magazine*, the "finest" moments designed
for fans of the Cartoon Network show!

EPIC MAD

By: The Usual Gang Of Idiots
ISBN: 978-1-4012-3762-2 | Diamond Code: DEC118177 | Price: $12.99 | Format: TP

Your favorite *MAD Magazine* parodies and segments available in one low-priced digest.

EXTREMELY MORONIC MAD

By: The Usual Gang Of Idiots
ISBN: 978-1-4012-3861-2 | Diamond Code: JUL120238 | Price: $12.99 | Format: TP

More "scrubbed clean" hilarity from *MAD*!

INSANELY AWESOME MAD

By: The Usual Gang Of Idiots
ISBN: 978-1-4012-3348-8 | Diamond Code: JUN110335 | Price: $12.99 | Format: TP

Insane, awesome and insanely awesome "best-of" features from *MAD*!

SPY VS. SPY: THE TOP SECRET FILES

By: Peter Kuper
ISBN: 978-1-4012-3527-7 | Diamond Code: AUG118124 | Price: $9.99 | Format: TP

The further misadventures of Spy vs. Spy by writer/artist Peter Kuper.

THE SPY VS. SPY OMNIBUS

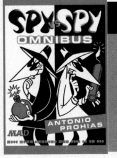

By: Antonio Prohias
ISBN: 978-1-4012-3237-5 | Diamond Code: JUL110276 | Price: $49.99 | Format: HC

Every Spy adventure ever written and drawn by its creator, Antonio Prohias.

DC: ALL AGES

All-ages graphic novels ranging from the crime-fighting team-ups in THE ALL NEW BATMAN: THE BRAVE AND THE BOLD to the teen heroics of YOUNG JUSTICE to the playground escapades of TINY TITANS!

TINY TITANS: WELCOME TO THE TREEHOUSE

Written and illustrated by Art Baltazar and Franco
ISBN: 978-1-4012-2078-5 | Diamond Code: NOV080197 | Price: $12.99 | Format: TP

Collects issues #1-6.

TINY TITANS: ADVENTURES IN AWESOMENESS

Written and illustrated by Art Baltazar and Franco
ISBN: 978-1-4012-2328-1 | Diamond Code: FEB090225 | Price: $12.99 | Format: TP

Collects issues #7-12.

TINY TITANS: SIDEKICKIN' IT

Written and illustrated by Art Baltazar and Franco
ISBN: 978-1-4012-2653-4 | Diamond Code: NOV090199 | Price: $12.99 | Format: TP

Collects issues #13-18.

TINY TITANS: THE FIRST RULE OF PET CLUB...

Written and illustrated by Art Baltazar and Franco
ISBN: 978-1-4012-2892-7 | Diamond Code: JUN100232 | Price: $12.99 | Format: TP

Collects issues #19-25.

TINY TITANS: FIELD TRIPPIN'

Written and illustrated by Art Baltazar and Franco
ISBN: 978-1-4012-3173-6 | Diamond Code: FEB110238 | Price: $12.99 | Format: TP

Collects issues #26-32.

TINY TITANS: THE TREEHOUSE AND BEYOND!

Written and illustrated by Art Baltazar & Franco
ISBN: 978-1-4012-3310-5 | Diamond Code: SEP110204 | Price: $12.99 | Format: TP

Collects issues #33-38.

TINY TITANS: GROWING UP TINY!

Written and illustrated by Art Baltazar & Franco
ISBN: 978-1-4012-3525-3 | Diamond Code: MAR120269 | Price: $12.99 | Format: TP
Collects issues #39-44.

YOUNG JUSTICE VOL. 1

Writers: Art Baltazar & Franco | Artists: Mike Norton & Christopher Jones
ISBN: 978-1-4012-3357-0 | Diamond Code: OCT110271 | Price: $12.99 | Format: TP

Based on the hit Cartoon Network show! Collects issues #0-6.

YOUNG JUSTICE VOL. 2: TRAINING DAY

Writers: Greg Weisman & Kevin Hopps | Artists: Dan Davis & Christopher Jones
ISBN: 978-1-4012-3748-6 | Diamond Code: AUG120274 | Price: $12.99 | Format: TP

Collects issues #7-13.

THE ALL-NEW BATMAN: THE BRAVE AND THE BOLD VOL. 1

Writer: Sholly Fisch | Artist: Rick Burchett
ISBN: 978-1-4012-3272-6 | Diamond Code: JUN110329 | Price: $12.99 | Format: TP

Spinning out of the Cartoon Network series comes the further adventures
of the Caped Crusader!

DC COMICS READING ORDER

SERIES # OR IMPRINT	ISBN	DIAMOND CODE	TITLE	AUTHOR	ARTIST	US$/ FORMAT
			BATMAN BACKLIST AND SUGGESTED READING ORDER			
1	9781401204440	FEB050257	BATMAN: THE GREATEST STORIES EVER TOLD	VARIOUS	VARIOUS	$19.99/TP
2	9781401212148	NOV060181	BATMAN: THE GREATEST STORIES EVER TOLD, VOL. 2	THOMAS, ROY	VARIOUS	$19.99/TP
3	9781401232948	AUG110254	TALES OF THE BATMAN: DON NEWTON	VARIOUS	NEWTON, DON	$39.99/HC
4	9781401231019	MAR110346	TALES OF THE BATMAN: GENE COLAN VOL. 1	VARIOUS	COLAN, GENE	$39.99/HC
5	9781401235376	MAR120248	BATMAN: ILLUSTRATED BY NEAL ADAMS VOL. 1	VARIOUS	ADAMS, NEAL	$24.99/HC
6	9781401236816	JUN120241	LEGENDS OF THE DARK KNIGHT: ALAN DAVIS	BARR, MIKE W.	DAVIS, ALAN	$39.99/HC
7	9781401233754	DEC110283	LEGENDS OF THE DARK KNIGHT: JIM APARO VOL. 1	HANEY, BOB	APARO, JIM	$29.99/HC
8	9781401232276	JUN110268	LEGENDS OF THE DARK KNIGHT: MARSHALL ROGERS	ENGLEHART, STEVE	ROGERS, MARSHALL	$49.99/HC
9	9781401204457	JAN050275	BATMAN CHRONICLES VOL. 1	FINGER, BILL	KANE, BOB	$14.99/TP
10	9781401207526	OCT060163	BATMAN: YEAR ONE	MILLER, FRANK	MAZZUCCHELLI, DAVID	$14.99/TP
11	9781401216269	SEP080167	BATMAN: THE MAN WHO LAUGHS	BRUBAKER, ED	MAHNKE, DOUG	$14.99/TP
12	9781401232597	JUL110251	BATMAN: THE LONG HALLOWEEN	LOEB, JEPH	SALE, TIM	$24.99/TP
13	0781563898686	MAR058151	BATMAN: DARK VICTORY	LOEB, JEPH	SALE, TIM	$19.99/TP
14	9781563892738	APR058324	BATMAN: HAUNTED KNIGHT	LOEB, JEPH	SALE, TIM	$14.99/TP
15	9781401201876	APR050327	BATMAN/SUPERMAN/WONDER WOMAN: TRINITY	WAGNER, MATT	WAGNER, MATT	$17.99/TP
16	9781401235154	FEB120260	BATMAN: PREY	MOENCH, DOUG	GULACY, PAUL	$24.99/TP
17	9781401232740	JUN110267	BATMAN: A DEATH IN THE FAMILY	STARLIN, JIM	APARO, JIM	$24.99/TP
18	9781401215491	JUN070170	BATMAN: GOTHIC	MORRISON, GRANT	JANSON, KLAUS	$14.99/TP
19	9781401204259	AUG050185	BATMAN: ARKHAM ASYLUM	MORRISON, GRANT	MCKEAN, DAVE	$17.99/TP
20	9781401216672	NOV070226	BATMAN: THE KILLING JOKE	MOORE, ALAN	BOLLAND, BRIAN	$17.99/HC
21	9781401233839	JAN120305	BATMAN: VENOM	O'NEIL, DENNIS J.	GARCIA-LOPEZ, JOSE LUIS	$14.99/TP
22	9781401233776	NOV110183	BATMAN VERSUS BANE	DIXON, CHUCK	NOLAN, GRAHAM	$12.99/TP
23	9781401233792	JAN120303	BATMAN: KNIGHTFALL VOL. 1	VARIOUS	VARIOUS	$29.99/TP
24	9781401235369	FEB120266	BATMAN: KNIGHTFALL VOL. 2	VARIOUS	VARIOUS	$29.99/TP
25	9781401237219	JUN120242	BATMAN: KNIGHTFALL VOL. 3	VARIOUS	VARIOUS	$29.99/TP
26	9781401232283	AUG110242	BATMAN: NO MAN'S LAND VOL. 1	VARIOUS	VARIOUS	$29.99/TP
27	9781401233808	JAN120304	BATMAN: NO MAN'S LAND VOL. 2	VARIOUS	VARIOUS	$29.99/TP
28	9781401234560	MAY120289	BATMAN: NO MAN'S LAND VOL. 3	VARIOUS	VARIOUS	$34.99/TP
29	9781401235642	SEP120237	BATMAN: NO MAN'S LAND VOL. 4	VARIOUS	VARIOUS	$34.99/TP
30	9781401223175	MAY090178	BATMAN: HUSH	LOEB, JEPH	LEE, JIM	$24.99/TP
31	9781401231453	MAY110241	BATMAN: UNDER THE RED HOOD	WINICK, JUDD	MAHNKE, DOUG	$29.99/TP
32	9781401231644	MAR110343	BATMAN: RED HOOD: LOST DAYS	WINICK, JUDD	VARIOUS	$14.99/TP
33	9781401212414	FEB128078	BATMAN & SON	MORRISON, GRANT	KUBERT, ANDY	$14.99/TP
34	9781401220327	FEB090202	BATMAN: THE RESURRECTION RA'S AL GHUL	VARIOUS	VARIOUS	$19.99/TP
35	9781401233365	FEB120256	BATMAN VS. THE BLACK GLOVE DELUXE EDITION	MORRISON, GRANT	WILLIAMS III, J.H.	$29.99/HC
36	9781401225766	MAR100237	BATMAN: R.I.P.	MORRISON, GRANT	DANIEL TONY S.	$14.99/TP

DC COMICS READING ORDER

SERIES # OR IMPRINT	ISBN	DIAMOND CODE	TITLE	AUTHOR	ARTIST	US$/ FORMAT
36	9781401221249	DEC090202	BATMAN: HEART OF HUSH	DINI, PAUL	NGUYEN, DUSTIN	$14.99/TP
37	9781401222826	MAR100239	FINAL CRISIS	MORRISON, GRANT	JONES, J.G.	$19.99/TP
38	9781401227241	APR100218	BATMAN: WHATEVER HAPPENED TO THE CAPED CRUSADER?	GAIMAN, NEIL	KUBERT, ANDY	$14.99/TP
39	9781401224172	AUG100188	BATMAN: BATTLE FOR THE COWL	DANIEL, TONY S.	DANIEL, TONY S.	$14.99/TP
40	9781401227203	FEB110195	BATMAN: LONG SHADOWS	WINICK, JUDD	BAGELY, MARK	$14.99/TP
41	9781401227227	FEB110196	BATMAN: STREETS OF GOTHAM VOL. 1: HUSH MONEY	DINI, PAUL	NGUYEN, DUSTIN	$14.99/TP
42	9781401229061	AUG110246	BATMAN: STREETS OF GOTHAM VOL. 2: LEVIATHAN	DINI, PAUL	NGUYEN, DUSTIN	$17.99/TP
43	9781401229870	DEC100246	BATMAN & ROBIN VOL. 1: BATMAN REBORN	MORRISON, GRANT	QUITELY, FRANK	$14.99/TP
44	9781401232719	AUG110241	BATMAN & ROBIN VOL. 2: BATMAN VS. ROBIN	MORRISON, GRANT	STEWART, CAMERON	$17.99/TP
45	9781401235086	FEB120258	BATMAN & ROBIN VOL. 3: BATMAN & ROBIN MUST DIE!	MORRISON, GRANT	FRAZER, IRVING	$17.99/TP
46	9781401235390	OCT120260	BATMAN & ROBIN VOL. 4: DARK KNIGHT, WHITE KNIGHT	VARIOUS	VARIOUS	$16.99/TP
47	9781401233822	OCT110245	BATMAN: THE RETURN OF BRUCE WAYNE	MORRISON, GRANT	PAQUETTE, YANICK	$19.99/TP
48	9781401233471	FEB120259	BATMAN: BRUCE WAYNE - THE ROAD HOME	VARIOUS	VARIOUS	$17.99/TP
49	9781401229757	JUL110250	BATMAN: LIFE AFTER DEATH	DANIEL, TONY S.	DANIEL, TONY S.	$14.99/TP
50	9781401229900	NOV110198	BATMAN: TIME AND THE BATMAN	MORRISON, GRANT	VARIOUS	$14.99/TP
51	9781401238278	DEC110261	BATMAN INCORPORATED VOL. 1 DELUXE EDITION	MORRISON, GRANT	PAQUETTE, YANICK	$19.99/TP
52	9781401230715	MAR110340	BATMAN: KNIGHT AND SQUIRE	CORNELL, PAUL	BROXTON, JIMMY	$14.99/TP
53	9781401234706	JUL120220	BATMAN: EYE OF THE BEHOLDER	DANIEL, TONY S.	DANIEL, TONY S.	$14.99/TP
54	9781401238285	OCT120261	BATMAN: THE DARK KNIGHT: GOLDEN DAWN	FINCH, DAVID	FINCH, DAVID	$14.99/TP
55	9781401233419	NOV110194	BATMAN: GATES OF GOTHAM	SNYDER, SCOTT	MCCARTHY, TREVOR	$14.99/TP
56	9781401232078	NOV120268	BATMAN: THE BLACK MIRROR	SNYDER, SCOTT	JOCK	$16.99/TP
57	9781401233389	DEC110276	FLASHPOINT	JOHNS, GEOFF	KUBERT, ANDY	$14.99/TP
58	9781401234058	DEC110277	FLASHPOINT: WORLD OF FLASHPOINT FEATURING BATMAN	AZZARELLO, BRIAN	RISSO, EDUARDO	$17.99/TP
59	9781401235420	DEC120323	BATMAN VOL. 1: THE COURT OF OWLS (THE NEW 52)	SNYDER, SCOTT	CAPULLO, GREG	$16.99/TP
60	9781401234676	JAN130296	BATMAN: DETECTIVE COMICS VOL. 1: FACES OF DEATH (THE NEW 52)	DANIEL, TONY S.	DANIEL, TONY	$16.99/TP
61	9781401235437	JUN120234	BATMAN: THE DARK KNIGHT VOL. 1: KNIGHT TERRORS (THE NEW 52)	FINCH, DAVID	FINCH, DAVID	$24.99/HC
62	9781401234874	MAR120241	BATMAN & ROBIN VOL. 1: BORN TO KILL (THE NEW 52)	TOMASI, PETER J.	GLEASON, PATRICK	$14.99/TP
63	9781401234768	APR120246	BATWING VOL. 1: THE LOST KINGDOM (THE NEW 52)	WINICK, JUDD	OLIVER, BEN	$14.99/TP
64	9781401232085	MAR120234	BATMAN: EARTH ONE	JOHNS, GEOFF	FRANK, GARY	$22.99/HC
65	9781401236762	JUL120219	BATMAN/JUDGE DREDD COLLECTION	WAGNER, JOHN	VARIOUS	$29.99/HC
66	9781401236830	MAY120287	BATMAN: ODYSSEY	ADAMS, NEAL	ADAMS, NEAL	$29.99/HC
67	9781401220082	MAR090174	ALL-STAR BATMAN & ROBIN, THE BOY WONDER VOL. 1	MILLER, FRANK	LEE, JIM	$19.99/TP
68	9781401231842	FEB110210	PLANETARY/BATMAN	ELLIS, WARREN	CASSADAY, JOHN	$22.99/HC
69	9781401215897	JUN070171	BATMAN: BLACK & WHITE VOL. 1	VARIOUS	VARIOUS	$19.99/TP
70	9781563899171	JUN060234	BATMAN: BLACK & WHITE VOL. 2	VARIOUS	VARIOUS	$19.99/TP
71	9781401213541	JUN080235	BATMAN: BLACK & WHITE VOL. 3	VARIOUS	VARIOUS	$19.99/TP

DC COMICS READING ORDER

SERIES # OR IMPRINT	ISBN	DIAMOND CODE	TITLE	AUTHOR	ARTIST	US$/ FORMAT
72	9781401215811	JUL080124	JOKER	AZZARELLO, BRIAN	BERMEJO, LEE	$18.98/HC
73	9781401211929	JAN130309	BATMAN: YEAR 100	POPE, PAUL	POPE, PAUL	$19.99/TP
74	9781563893421	NOV118085	BATMAN: THE DARK KNIGHT RETURNS	MILLER, FRANK	MILLER, FRANK	$14.99/TP
75	9781563899294	FEB058404	BATMAN: THE DARK KNIGHT STRIKES AGAIN	MILLER, FRANK	MILLER, FRANK	$18.99/TP
76	9781401234835	JUN120243	BATMAN: ARKHAM CITY	DINI, PAUL	D'ANDA, CARLOS	$16.99/TP
77	9781401237493	OCT120263	BATMAN: ARKHAM UNHINGED	FRIDOLFS, DEREK	MILLER, MIKE S.	$22.99/HC
78	9781401234539	JAN120285	BATMAN: DEATH BY DESIGN	KIDD, CHIP	TAYLOR, DAVE	$24.99/TP
79	9781401213586	AUG080177	BATMAN: EGO AND OTHER TAILS	COOKE, DARWYN	COOKE, DARWYN	$17.99/TP
80	9781401222284	NOV080172	BATMAN: FALSE FACES	VAUGHAN, BRIAN K.	MCDANIEL, SCOTT	$14.99/TP
81	9781401224189	JUN100204	BATMAN: CACOPHONY	SMITH, KEVIN	FLANAGAN, WALT	$14.99/TP
82	9781401228767	JUN110270	BATMAN: THE WIDENING GYRE	SMITH, KEVIN	FLANAGAN, WALT	$17.99/TP
83	9781401232139	JUL110245	BATMAN: NOEL	BERMEJO, LEE	BERMEJO, LEE	$22.99/HC
84	9781401233815	DEC110282	BATMAN: BIRTH OF THE DEMON	BARR, MIKE W.	VARIOUS	$29.99/TP

SUPERMAN BACKLIST AND SUGGESTED READING ORDER

SERIES # OR IMPRINT	ISBN	DIAMOND CODE	TITLE	AUTHOR	ARTIST	US$/ FORMAT
1	9781401203399	NOV058069	SUPERMAN: THE GREATEST STORIES EVER TOLD	VARIOUS	VARIOUS	$19.99/TP
2	9781401207649	NOV050250	SUPERMAN CHRONICLES VOL. 1	SIEGEL, JERRY	SHUSTER, JOE	$14.99/TP
3	9781401204563	FEB050263	SUPERMAN VS. THE FLASH	VARIOUS	VARIOUS	$19.99/TP
4	9781401218406	JUL080169	SUPERMAN VS. BRAINIAC	VARIOUS	VARIOUS	$19.99/TP
5	9781401227319	APR100219	SUPERMAN: WHATEVER HAPPENED TO THE MAN OF TOMORROW?	MOORE, ALAN	SWAN, CURT	$14.99/TP
6	9780930289287	JUL058226	SUPERMAN: MAN OF STEEL VOL. 1	BYRNE, JOHN	BYRNE, JOHN	$14.99/TP
7	9781401200053	MAR068126	SUPERMAN: MAN OF STEEL VOL. 2	BYRNE, JOHN	BYRNE, JOHN	$19.99/TP
8	9781401202460	JUL088086	SUPERMAN: MAN OF STEEL VOL. 3	BYRNE, JOHN	BYRNE, JOHN	$19.99/TP
9	9781401204556	JUN050349	SUPERMAN: MAN OF STEEL VOL. 4	BYRNE, JOHN	BYRNE, JOHN	$19.99/TP
10	9781401209483	AUG060185	SUPERMAN: MAN OF STEEL VOL. 5	BYRNE, JOHN	BYRNE, JOHN	$19.99/TP
11	9781401216795	DEC070254	SUPERMAN: MAN OF STEEL VOL. 6	BYRNE, JOHN	BYRNE, JOHN	$19.99/TP
12	9781563895296	FEB088194	SUPERMAN: FOR ALL SEASONS	LOEB, JEPH	SALE, TIM	$17.99/TP
13	9781401241827	OCT120269	THE DEATH OF SUPERMAN	VARIOUS	VARIOUS	$14.99/TP
14	9781563891182	MAY108143	A WORLD WITHOUT SUPERMAN	VARIOUS	VARIOUS	$19.99/TP
15	9781563891496	OCT058018	THE RETURN OF SUPERMAN	VARIOUS	VARIOUS	$19.99/TP
16	9781401229306	JUN100212	LUTHOR	AZZARELLO, BRIAN	BERMEJO, LEE	$18.99/HC
17	9781401237806	NOV120270	SUPERMAN: FOR TOMORROW	AZZARELLO, BRIAN	LEE, JIM	$24.99/TP
18	9781401212056	MAR080188	SUPERMAN: CAMELOT FALLS VOL.1	BUSIEK, KURT	PACHECO, CARLOS	$12.99/TP
19	9781401218652	NOV080181	SUPERMAN: CAMELOT FALLS VOL.2	BUSIEK, KURT	PACHECO, CARLOS	$12.99/TP
20	9781401221324	JAN100300	SUPERMAN: COMING OF ATLAS	ROBINSON, JAMES	GUEDES, RENATO	$14.99/TP
21	9781401232883	SEP110188	SUPERMAN: SECRET ORIGIN	JOHNS, GEOFF	FRANK, GARY	$19.99/TP
22	9781401237790	OCT120270	SUPERMAN: LAST SON OF KRYPTON	JOHNS, GEOFF	KUBERT, ADAM	$19.99/TP

DC COMICS READING ORDER

SERIES # OR IMPRINT	ISBN	DIAMOND CODE	TITLE	AUTHOR	ARTIST	US$/FORMAT
23	9781401220334	FEB090217	SUPERMAN: ESCAPE FROM BIZARRO WORLD	JOHNS, GEOFF	POWELL, ERIC	$14.99/TP
24	9781401219048	APR090217	SUPERMAN AND THE LEGION OF SUPER-HEROES	JOHNS, GEOFF	FRANK, GARY	$14.99/TP
25	9781401209544	JUN060169	SUPERMAN : UP, UP & AWAY	JOHNS, GEOFF	WOODS, PETE	$14.99/TP
26	9781401230760	FEB120265	SUPERMAN: GROUNDED VOL. 1	STRACZYNSKI, MICHAEL J.	BARROWS, EDDY	$17.99/TP
27	9781401235321	SEP120241	SUPERMAN: GROUNDED VOL. 2	STRACZYNSKI, J. MICHAEL	BARROWS, EDDY	$14.99/TP
28	9781401230340	NOV110203	SUPERMAN: THE BLACK RING VOL. 1	CORNEL, PAUL	WOODS, PETE	$14.99/TP
29	9781401234447	JUN120255	SUPERMAN: THE BLACK RING VOL. 2	CORNELL, PAUL	WOODS, PETE	$16.99/TP
30	9781401232535	AUG110260	SUPERMAN: THE RETURN OF DOOMSDAY	VARIOUS	VARIOUS	$14.99/TP
31	9781401236885	DEC120340	SUPERMAN: THE REIGN OF DOOMSDAY	CORNELL, PAUL	ROCAFORT, KENNETH	$16.99/TP
32	9781401235475	FEB130215	SUPERMAN: ACTION COMICS VOL. 1: SUPERMAN AND THE MEN OF STEEL (THE NEW 52)	MORRISON, GRANT	MORALES, RAGS	$16.99/TP
33	9781401234683	JUL120210	SUPERMAN VOL. 1: WHAT PRICE TOMORROW? (THE NEW 52)	PEREZ, GEORGE	MERINO, JESUS	$22.99/HC
34	9781401201876	APR050327	BATMAN/SUPERMAN/WONDER WOMAN: TRINITY	WAGNER, MATT	WAGNER, MATT	$17.99/TP
35	9781401202200	JUL090239	SUPERMAN/BATMAN: PUBLIC ENEMIES VOL. 1	LOEB, JEPH	MCGUINNESS, ED	$14.99/TP
36	9781401202507	SEP098202	SUPERMAN/BATMAN: SUPERGIRL VOL. 2	LOEB, JEPH	TURNER, MICHAEL	$14.99/TP
37	9781401207144	AUG060184	SUPERMAN/BATMAN: ABSOLUTE POWER VOL. 3	LOEB, JEPH	PACHECO, CARLOS	$12.99/TP
38	9781401210434	AUG080185	SUPERMAN/BATMAN: VENGEANCE VOL. 4	LOEB, JEPH	MCGUINNESS, ED	$12.99/TP
39	9781401212438	DEC080164	SUPERMAN/BATMAN: THE ENEMIES AMONG US	VERHEIDEN, MARK	VAN SCIVER, ETHAN	$12.99/TP
40	9781401217402	NOV100234	SUPERMAN/BATMAN: TORMENT	BURNETT, ALAN	NGUYEN, DUSTIN	$14.99/TP
41	9781401228088	MAY110252	SUPERMAN/BATMAN: NIGHT & DAY	GREEN, MICHAEL	KOLINS, SCOTT	$17.99/TP
42	9781401229146	SEP100256	SUPERMAN/BATMAN: BIG NOISE	CASEY, JOE	KOLINS, SCOTT	$14.99/TP
43	9781401230326	JAN110333	SUPERMAN/BATMAN: WORSHIP	LEVITZ, PAUL	GUEDES, RENATO	$17.99/TP
44	9781401234461	JUL120227	SUPERMAN/BATMAN: SORCERER KINGS	BUNN, CULLEN	CHRISCROSS	$14.99/TP
45	9781401222772	MAR090192	TRINITY VOL. 1	BUSIEK, KURT	BAGLEY, MARK	$29.99/TP
46	9781401223182	MAY090196	TRINITY VOL. 2	BUSIEK, KURT	BAGLEY, MARK	$29.99/TP
47	9781401223571	JUL090243	TRINITY VOL. 3	BUSIEK, KURT	BAGLEY, MARK	$29.99/TP
48	9781401224691	FEB130226	SUPERMAN: EARTH ONE VOL. 1	STRACZYNSKI, J. MICHAEL	DAVIS, SHANE	$12.99/TP
49	9781401231965	JUN120225	SUPERMAN: EARTH ONE VOL. 2	STRACZYNSKI, J. MICHAEL	DAVIS, SHANE	$22.99/HC
50	9781401202521	JUL050214	SUPERMAN: BIRTHRIGHT	WAID, MARK	IMMONEN, STUART	$19.99/TP
51	9781401232054	JUL110247	ALL-STAR SUPERMAN	MORRISON, GRANT	QUITELY, FRANK	$29.99/TP
52	9781401228415	APR100224	SUPERMAN VS. MUHAMMAD ALI DELUXE EDITION	O'NEIL, DENNIS	ADAMS, NEAL	$19.99/HC
53	9781401201813	NOV058130	SUPERMAN: RED SON	MILLAR, MARK	JOHNSON, DAVE	$17.99/TP

GREEN LANTERN BACKLIST AND SUGGESTED READING ORDER

SERIES # OR IMPRINT	ISBN	DIAMOND CODE	TITLE	AUTHOR	ARTIST	US$/FORMAT
1	9781401208612	MAY060165	GREEN LANTERN: THE GREATEST STORIES EVER TOLD	VARIOUS	VARIOUS	$16.99/TP
2	9781401219864	JUL080158	GREEN LANTERN: IN BRIGHTEST DAY	BROOME, JOHN	KANE, GIL	$19.99/TP
3	9781401221638	JAN090229	GREEN LANTERN CHRONICLES VOL. 1	BROOME, JOHN	KANE, GIL	$14.99/TP
4	9781401233969	DEC110285	GREEN LANTERN CHRONICLES VOL. 4	BROOME, JOHN	KANE, GIL	$14.99/TP

SERIES # OR IMPRINT	ISBN	DIAMOND CODE	TITLE	AUTHOR	ARTIST	US$/ FORMAT
5	9781401235178	MAY120290	GREEN LANTERN/GREEN ARROW	O'NEIL, DENNIS	ADAMS, NEAL	$29.99/TP
6	9781401236892	AUG120252	GREEN LANTERN: SECTOR 2814 VOL. 1	WEIN, LEN	GIBBONS, DAVE	$16.99/TP
7	9781563891847	JUN068105	ZERO HOUR: CRISIS IN TIME	JURGENS, DAN	JURGENS, DAN	$17.99/TP
8	9781401227555	FEB100185	GREEN LANTERN: REBIRTH	JOHNS, GEOFF	VAN SCIVER, ETHAN	$14.99/TP
9	9781401210588	FEB080244	GREEN LANTERN: NO FEAR	JOHNS, GEOFF	PACHECO, CARLOS	$12.99/TP
10	9781401209605	JUN088401	GREEN LANTERN: REVENGE OF THE GREEN LANTERNS	JOHNS, GEOFF	PACHECO, CARLOS	$14.99/TP
11	9781401215903	OCT080170	GREEN LANTERN: WANTED: HAL JORDAN	JOHNS, GEOFF	REIS, IVAN	$29.99/TP
12	9781401233013	JUN110275	GREEN LANTERN: THE SINESTRO CORPS WAR	JOHNS, GEOFF	REIS, IVAN	$29.99/TP
13	9781401223267	MAR090178	GREEN LANTERNS: TALES OF THE SINESTRO CORPS	VARIOUS	VARIOUS	$14.99/TP
14	9781401230860	JAN110337	GREEN LANTERN: SECRET ORIGIN	JOHNS, GEOFF	REIS, IVAN	$14.99/TP
15	9781401223021	APR100214	GREEN LANTERN: RAGE OF THE RED LANTERNS	JOHNS, GEOFF	REIS, IVAN	$14.99/TP
16	9781401224202	AUG100204	GREEN LANTERN: AGENT ORANGE	JOHNS, GEOFF	TAN, PHILIP	$14.99/TP
17	9781401228064	APR110195	BLACKEST NIGHT: RISE OF THE BLACK LANTERNS	VARIOUS	VARIOUS	$19.99/TP
18	9781401228071	APR110196	BLACKEST NIGHT: TALES OF THE CORPS	VARIOUS	VARIOUS	$19.99/TP
19	9781401229535	APR110192	BLACKEST NIGHT	JOHNS, GEOFF	REIS, IVAN	$19.99/TP
20	9781401228528	APR110193	BLACKEST NIGHT: GREEN LANTERN	JOHNS, GEOFF	MAHNKE, DOUG	$19.99/TP
21	9781401228057	APR110194	BLACKEST NIGHT: GREEN LANTERN CORPS	TOMASI, PETER J.	GLEASON, PATRICK	$19.99/TP
22	9781401228040	APR110197	BLACKEST NIGHT: BLACK LANTERN CORPS VOL. 1	VARIOUS	VARIOUS	$19.99/TP
23	9781401228033	APR110198	BLACKEST NIGHT: BLACK LANTERN CORPS VOL. 2	VARIOUS	VARIOUS	$19.99/TP
24	9781401232764	SEP110177	BRIGHTEST DAY VOL. 1	JOHNS, GEOFF	REIS, IVAN	$19.99/TP
25	9781401230845	FEB120255	BRIGHTEST DAY VOL. 2	JOHNS, GEOFF	REIS, IVAN	$19.99/TP
26	9781401232177	JUN120244	BRIGHTEST DAY VOL. 3	JOHNS, GEOFF	REIS, IVAN	$16.99/TP
27	9781401231415	FEB120254	GREEN LANTERN: BRIGHEST DAY	JOHNS, GEOFF	MAHNKE, DOUG	$19.99/TP
28	9781401234522	JUN120246	GREEN LANTERN: WAR OF THE GREEN LANTERNS	VARIOUS	VARIOUS	$16.99/TP
29	9781401235363	OCT120265	WAR OF THE GREEN LANTERNS: AFTERMATH	BEDARD, TONY	VARIOUS	$16.99/TP
30	9781401234065	DEC110280	FLASHPOINT: THE WORLD OF FLASHPOINT FEATURING GREEN LANTERN	VARIOUS	VARIOUS	$17.99/TP
31	9781401234553	OCT120257	GREEN LANTERN VOL. 1: SINESTRO (THE NEW 52)	JOHNS, GEOFF	MAHNKE, DOUG	$14.99/TP
32	9781401221553	NOV080187	TALES OF GREEN LANTERN CORPS VOL. 1	VARIOUS	VARIOUS	$19.99/TP
33	9781401227029	OCT080254	TALES OF GREEN LANTERN CORPS VOL. 2	VARIOUS	VARIOUS	$19.99/TP
34	9781401229344	SEP100259	TALES OF GREEN LANTERN CORPS VOL. 3	VARIOUS	VARIOUS	$19.99/TP
35	9781401209629	AUG038004	GREEN LANTERN CORPS: RECHARGE	JOHNS, GEOFF	GLEASON, PATRICK	$14.99/TP
36	9781401213565	AUG098053	GREEN LANTERN CORPS: TO BE A LANTERN	GIBBONS, DAVE	GLEASON, PATRICK	$14.99/TP
37	9781401215071	AUG070273	GREEN LANTERN CORPS: DARK SIDE	GIBBONS, DAVE	GLEASON, PATRICK	$12.99/TP
38	9781401222734	MAR080182	GREEN LANTERN CORPS: SINS OF THE STAR SAPPHIRE	TOMASI, PETER J.	GLEASON, PATRICK	$14.99/TP
39	9781401219758	AUG080181	GREEN LANTERN CORPS: RING QUEST	TOMASI, PETER J.	GLEASON, PATRICK	$14.99/TP
40	9781401225292	AUG100205	GREEN LANTERN CORPS: EMERALD ECLIPSE	TOMASI, PETER J.	GLEASON, PATRICK	$14.99/TP

DC COMICS READING ORDER

SERIES # OR IMPRINT	ISBN	DIAMOND CODE	TITLE	AUTHOR	ARTIST	US$/ FORMAT
41	9781401231408	MAR120252	GREEN LANTERN CORPS: REVOLT OF THE ALPHA LANTERNS	BEDARD, TONY	SYAF, ARDIAN	$14.99/TP
42	9781401230807	APR120252	GREEN LANTERN: EMERALD WARRIORS VOL. 1	TOMASI, PETER J.	PASARIN, FERNANDO	$14.99/TP
43	9781401234416	JUL120222	GREEN LANTERN CORPS: THE WEAPONER	BEDARD, TONY	KIRKHAM, TYLER	$14.99/TP
44	9781401237011	MAY120278	GREEN LANTERN CORPS VOL. 1: FEARSOME (THE NEW 52)	TOMASI, PETER J.	PASARIN, FERNANDO	$22.99/HC
45	9781401237073	JUN120235	GREEN LANTERN: NEW GUARDIANS VOL. 1: THE RING BEARER (THE NEW 52)	BEDARD, TONY	KIRKHAM, TYLER	$22.99/HC
46	9781401234911	MAR120243	RED LANTERNS VOL. 1: BLOOD AND RAGE (THE NEW 52)	MILLIGAN, PETER	BENES, ED	$14.99/TP

THE FLASH BACKLIST AND SUGGESTED READING ORDER

1	9781401224974	AUG090173	FLASH VS THE ROGUES	BROOME, JOHN	INFANTINO, CARMINE	$14.99/TP
2	9781401230685	JAN110328	THE FLASH OMNIBUS BY GEOFF JOHNS VOL. 1	JOHNS, GEOFF	VARIOUS	$75.00/HC
3	9781401233914	NOV110187	THE FLASH OMNIBUS BY GEOFF JOHNS VOL. 2	JOHNS, GEOFF	VARIOUS	$75.00/HC
4	9781401237172	APR120254	THE FLASH OMNIBUS BY GEOFF JOHNS VOL. 3	JOHNS, GEOFF	VARIOUS	$75.00/HC
5	9781401223342	APR100213	FINAL CRISIS: ROGUE'S REVENGE	JOHNS, GEOFF	KOLINS, SCOTT	$14.99/TP
6	9781401230012	JAN110329	THE FLASH: REBIRTH	JOHNS, GEOFF	VAN SCIVER, ETHAN	$14.99/TP
7	9781401226702	OCT100267	THE FLASH VOL. 1: THE DASTARDLY DEATH OF THE ROGUES!	JOHNS, GEOFF	MANAPUL, FRANCIS	$19.99/TP
8	9781401234485	JUN120245	THE FLASH VOL. 2: THE ROAD TO FLASHPOINT	JOHNS, GEOFF	MANAPUL, FRANCIS	$14.99/TP
9	9781401233389	DEC110276	FLASHPOINT	JOHNS, GEOFF	KUBERT, ANDY	$14.99/TP
10	9781401234058	DEC110277	FLASHPOINT: WORLD OF FLASHPOINT FEATURING BATMAN	VARIOUS	VARIOUS	$17.99/TP
11	9781401234065	DEC110280	FLASHPOINT: WORLD OF FLASHPOINT FEATURING GREEN LANTERN	VARIOUS	VARIOUS	$17.99/TP
12	9781401234102	DEC110279	FLASHPOINT: WORLD OF FLASHPOINT FEATURING WONDER WOMAN	VARIOUS	VARIOUS	$17.99/TP
13	9781401234089	DEC110281	FLASHPOINT: WORLD OF FLASHPOINT FEATURING THE FLASH	VARIOUS	VARIOUS	$17.99/TP
14	9781401234348	DEC110278	FLASHPOINT: WORLD OF FLASHPOINT FEATURING SUPERMAN	VARIOUS	VARIOUS	$17.99/TP
15	9781401235536	JUL120209	THE FLASH VOL. 1: MOVE FORWARD (THE NEW 52)	MANAPUL, FRANCIS	MANAPUL, FRANCIS	$24.99/HC

JUSTICE LEAGUE BACKLIST AND SUGGESTED READING ORDER

1	9781401208322	DEC050265	JLA: THE GREATEST STORIES EVER TOLD	VARIOUS	VARIOUS	$19.99/TP
2	9781401233143	JUN110276	JLA VOL. 1	MORRISON, GRANT	PORTER, HOWARD	$19.99/TP
3	9781401235185	APR120256	JLA VOL. 2	MORRISON, GRANT	PORTER, HOWARD	$24.99/TP
4	9781401238322	OCT120267	JLA VOL. 3	MORRISON, GRANT	PORTER, HOWARD	$24.99/TP
5	9781401229092	JUL100202	JLA VOL. 4	MORRISON, GRANT	PORTER, HOWARD	$34.99/HC
6	9781401240950	AUG120253	JLA: EARTH 2	MORRISON, GRANT	QUITELY, FRANK	$14.99/TP
7	9781401204587	AUG118125	IDENTITY CRISIS	MELTZER, BRAD	MORALES, RAGS	$17.99/TP
8	9781401215804	JUN080244	JUSTICE LEAGUE OF AMERICA: THE TORNADO'S PATH, VOL. 1	MELTZER, BRAD	BENES, ED	$17.99/TP
9	9781401218690	OCT080173	JUSTICE LEAGUE OF AMERICA: THE LIGHTNING SAGA, VOL. 2	MELTZER, BRAD	BENES, ED	$17.99/TP
10	9781401220501	MAR090190	JUSTICE LEAGUE OF AMERICA: THE INJUSTICE LEAGUE	MCDUFFIE, DWAYNE	BENES, ED	$17.99/TP
11	9781401220105	OCT090247	JUSTICE LEAGUE OF AMERICA: SANCTUARY	MCDUFFIE, DWAYNE	BENES, ED	$14.99/TP
12	9781401222536	FEB100187	JUSTICE LEAGUE OF AMERICA: THE SECOND COMING	MCDUFFIE, DWAYNE	BENES, ED	$17.99/TP
13	9781401224233	JUL100203	JUSTICE LEAGUE OF AMERICA: WHEN WORLDS COLLIDE	MCDUFFIE, DWAYNE	BENES, ED	$14.99/TP

DC COMICS READING ORDER

SERIES # OR IMPRINT	ISBN	DIAMOND CODE	TITLE	AUTHOR	ARTIST	US$/ FORMAT
14	9781401225643	MAR110353	JUSTICE LEAGUE: CRY FOR JUSTICE	ROBINSON, JAMES	CASCIOLI, MAURO	$19.99/TP
16	9781401230142	DEC110290	JUSTICE LEAGUE: RISE AND FALL	KRUL, J.T.	DALLOCCHIO, FEDERICO	$17.99/TP
17	9781401232603	JUN110277	JUSTICE LEAGUE OF AMERICA: TEAM HISTORY	ROBINSON, JAMES	BAGLEY, MARK	$17.99/TP
18	9781401231934	DEC110289	JUSTICE LEAGUE OF AMERICA: DARK THINGS	ROBINSON, JAMES	BAGLEY, MARK	$17.99/TP
19	9781401232436	MAY110247	JUSTICE LEAGUE OF AMERICA: OMEGA	ROBINSON, JAMES	BAGLEY, MARK	$24.99/TP
20	9781401234133	JUL120225	JUSTICE LEAGUE AMERICA: THE RISE OF ECLIPSO	ROBINSON, JAMES	BOOTH, BRETT	$22.99/TP
21	9781401237882	OCT120252	JUSTICE LEAGUE VOL. 1: ORIGIN (THE NEW 52)	JOHNS, GEOFF	LEE, JIM	$16.99/TP
22	9781401217396	DEC080163	JUSTICE LEAGUE INTERNATIONAL VOL. 1	GIFFEN, KEITH	MAGUIRE, KEVIN	$17.99/TP
23	9781401220204	APR090211	JUSTICE LEAGUE INTERNATIONAL VOL. 2	GIFFEN, KEITH	MAGUIRE, KEVIN	$17.99/TP
24	9781401225384	AUG090174	JUSTICE LEAGUE INTERNATIONAL VOL. 3	GIFFEN, KEITH	MAGUIRE, KEVIN	$19.99/TP
25	9781401221973	DEC090212	JUSTICE LEAGUE INTERNATIONAL VOL. 4	GIFFEN, KEITH	MAGUIRE, KEVIN	$17.99/TP
26	9781401230104	OCT100266	JUSTICE LEAGUE INTERNATIONAL VOL. 5	GIFFEN, KEITH	MAGUIRE, KEVIN	$19.99/TP
27	9781401230203	DEC100249	JUSTICE LEAGUE: GENERATION LOST VOL. 1	WINICK, JUDD	LOPRESTI, AARON	$39.99/HC
28	9781401232832	JUN110278	JUSTICE LEAGUE: GENERATION LOST VOL. 2	WINICK, JUDD	LOPRESTI, AARON	$39.99/HC
29	9781401236345	FEB120250	JUSTICE LEAGUE INTERNATIONAL VOL.1: THE SIGNAL MASTERS (THE NEW 52)	JURGENS, DAN	LOPRESTI, AARON	$14.99/TP
30	9781401237042	JUL120211	JUSTICE LEAGUE DARK VOL. 1: IN THE DARK (THE NEW 52)	MILLIGAN, PETER	JANIN, MIKEL	$14.99/TP
31	9781401203504	FEB058027	DC: THE NEW FRONTIER VOL. 1	COOKE, DARWYN	COOKE, DARWYN	$19.99/TP
32	9781401204817	FEB050272	DC: THE NEW FRONTIER VOL. 2	COOKE, DARWYN	COOKE, DARWYN	$19.99/TP
33	9781563894800	MAR045122	JUSTICE LEAGUE OF AMERICA: THE NAIL	DAVIS, ALAN	DAVIS, ALAN	$14.95/TP
34	9781401231859	MAR110354	JUSTICE	ROSS, ALEX	ROSS, ALEX	$39.99/TP
35	9781401220341	JUN080246	KINGDOM COME	WAID, MARK	ROSS, ALEX	$17.99/TP
36	9781563896678	APR068118	KINGDOM	WAID, MARK	VARIOUS	$19.99/TP

WONDER WOMAN BACKLIST AND SUGGESTED READING ORDER

1	9781401212162	JAN070323	WONDER WOMAN: THE GREATEST STORIES EVER TOLD	VARIOUS	VARIOUS	$19.99/TP
2	9781401234842	APR120250	WONDER WOMAN: TWELVE LABORS	VARIOUS	VARIOUS	$14.99/TP
3	9781401230784	OCT120256	WONDER WOMAN: ODYSSEY VOL. 1	STRACZYNSKI, J. MICHAEL	KRAMER, DON	$14.99/TP
4	9781401234324	NOV120274	WONDER WOMAN : ODYSSEY VOL. 2	STRACZYNSKI, J. MICHAEL	KRAMER, DON	$14.99/TP
5	9781401234102	DEC110279	FLASHPOINT: WORLD OF FLASHPOINT FEATURING WONDER WOMAN	VARIOUS	VARIOUS	$17.99/TP
6	9781401235628	OCT120256	WONDER WOMAN VOL. 1: BLOOD (THE NEW 52)	AZZARELLO, BRIAN	CHIANG, CLIFF	$14.99/TP

GREEN ARROW BACKLIST AND SUGGESTED READING ORDER

1	9781401231071	MAR110355	THE JACK KIRBY OMNIBUS VOL. 1	VARIOUS	KIRBY, JACK	$49.99/TP
2	9781401217433	JAN090227	GREEN ARROW: YEAR ONE	DIGGLE, ANDY	JOCK	$14.99/TP
3	9781401235178	MAY120290	GREEN LANTERN/GREEN ARROW	O'NEIL, DENNIS	ADAMS, NEAL	$29.99/TP
4	9781401238628	JUN120250	GREEN ARROW: THE LONGBOW HUNTERS	GRELL, MIKE	GRELL, MIKE	$14.99/TP
5	9781401200442	JUN120251	GREEN ARROW: THE ARCHER'S QUEST	MELTZER, BRAD	HESTER, PHIL	$14.99/TP
6	9781401230746	APR120253	GREEN ARROW: INTO THE WOODS VOL. 1	KRUL, J.T.	NEVES, DIOGENES	$14.99/TP

DC COMICS READING ORDER

SERIES # OR IMPRINT	ISBN	DIAMOND CODE	TITLE	AUTHOR	ARTIST	US$/ FORMAT
7	9781401235284	NOV120266	GREEN ARROW: SALVATION VOL. 2	KRUL, J.T.	NEVES, DIOGENES	$16.99/TP
8	9781401234867	FEB120248	GREEN ARROW VOL. 1: THE MIDAS TOUCH (THE NEW 52)	KRUL, J.T.	PEREZ, GEORGE	$14.99/TP

JUSTICE SOCIETY OF AMERICA BACKLIST AND SUGGESTED READING ORDER

SERIES # OR IMPRINT	ISBN	DIAMOND CODE	TITLE	AUTHOR	ARTIST	US$/ FORMAT
1	9781401215859	JUL080163	JUSTICE SOCIETY AMERICA: THE NEXT AGE	JOHNS, GEOFF	EAGLESHAM, DALE	$14.99/TP
2	9781401217419	JAN090231	JUSTICE SOCIETY OF AMERICA: THY KINGDOM COME PART I	JOHNS, GEOFF	EAGLESHAM, DALE	$14.99/TP
3	9781401218468	AUG090175	JUSTICE SOCIETY OF AMERICA: THY KINGDOM COME PART II	JOHNS, GEOFF	EAGLESHAM, DALE	$19.99/TP
4	9781401221676	JAN100298	JUSTICE SOCIETY OF AMERICA: THY KINGDOM COME PART III	JOHNS, GEOFF	EAGLESHAM, DALE	$19.99/TP
5	9781401225315	JUN100206	JUSTICE SOCIETY OF AMERICA: BLACK ADAM & ISIS	JOHNS, GEOFF	ORDWAY, JERRY	$14.99/TP
6	9781401227142	FEB100189	JUSTICE SOCIETY OF AMERICA: THE BAD SEED	WILLINGHAM, BILL	MERINO, JESÚS	$14.99/TP
7	9781401229016	SEP100251	JUSTICE SOCIETY OF AMERICA: AXIS OF EVIL	WILLINGHAM, BILL	MERINO, JESÚS	$14.99/TP
8	9781401232849	JUN110279	JUSTICE SOCIETY OF AMERICA: SUPERTOWN	GUGGENHEIM, MARC	KOLINS, SCOTT	$14.99/TP
9	9781401233686	NOV110205	JUSTICE SOCIETY OF AMERICA: MONUMENT PARK	GUGGENHEIM, MARC	DERENICK, TOM	$14.99/TP
10	9781401235000	MAR120247	MISTER TERRIFIC VOL. 1: MIND GAMES	WALLACE, ERIC	GUGLIOTTA, GIANLUCA	$14.99/TP

LEGION OF SUPER-HEROES BACKLIST AND SUGGESTED READING ORDER

SERIES # OR IMPRINT	ISBN	DIAMOND CODE	TITLE	AUTHOR	ARTIST	US$/ FORMAT
1	9781401237301	JUL120224	LEGION: SECRET ORIGIN	LEVITZ, PAUL	BATISTA, CHRIS	$14.99/TP
2	9781401230982	APR110207	LEGION OF SUPER-HEROES: THE CURSE DELUXE EDITION	VARIOUS	VARIOUS	$49.99/HC
3	9781401218444	SEP080174	LEGION OF SUPER-HEROES: THE MORE THINGS CHANGE	LEVITZ, PAUL	GIFFEN, KEITH	$17.99/TP
4	9781401231200	FEB110204	LEGION LOST	ABNETT, DAN	COIPEL, OLIVIER	$39.99/TP
5	9781401223250	JUL100185	FINAL CRISIS: LEGION OF 3 WORLDS	JOHNS, GEOFF	PEREZ, GEORGE	$14.99/TP
6	9781401231682	FEB110203	SUPERBOY AND THE LEGION OF SUPER-HEROES: EARLY YEARS	LEVITZ, PAUL	PANSICA, EDUARDO	$14.99/TP
7	9781401219048	APR090217	SUPERMAN AND THE LEGION OF SUPER-HEROES	JOHNS, GEOFF	FRANK, GARY	$14.99/TP
8	9781401220181	JUL080236	LEGION OF SUPER-HEROES: ENEMY RISING	SHOOTER, JIM	LOPRESTI, AARON	$14.99/TP
9	9781401223052	FEB100190	LEGION OF SUPER-HEROES: ENEMY MANIFEST	SHOOTER, JIM	MANAPUL, FRANCIS	$14.99/TP
10	9781401230385	DEC100250	LEGION OF SUPER-HEROES VOL. 1: THE CHOICE	LEVITZ, PAUL	CINAR, YILDIRAY	$24.99/TP
11	9781401232382	MAY110251	LEGION OF SUPER-HEROES VOL. 2: CONSEQUENCES	LEVITZ, PAUL	CINAR, YILDIRAY	$24.99/TP
12	9781401233679	JAN120311	LEGION OF SUPER-HEROES: WHEN EVIL CALLS	LEVITZ, PAUL	CINAR, YILDIRAY	$26.99/TP
13	9781401237035	JUN120238	LEGION LOST VOL. 1: RUN FROM TOMORROW (THE NEW 52)	NICIEZA, FABIAN	WOODS, PETE	$14.99/TP
14	9781401235017	MAR120246	LEGION OF SUPER-HEROES VOL. 1: HOSTILE WORLD (THE NEW 52)	LEVITZ, PAUL	PORTELA, FRANCIS	$14.99/TP

TEEN TITANS BACKLIST AND SUGGESTED READING ORDER

SERIES # OR IMPRINT	ISBN	DIAMOND CODE	TITLE	AUTHOR	ARTIST	US$/ FORMAT
1	9781401231088	APR110205	NEW TEEN TITANS OMNIBUS VOL. 1	WOLFMAN, MARV	PEREZ, GEORGE	$75.00/HC
2	9781401234284	DEC110282	NEW TEEN TITANS OMNIBUS VOL. 2	WOLFMAN, MARV	PEREZ, GEORGE	$75.00/HC
3	9781401203191	NOV120275	NEW TEEN TITANS: GAMES	WOLFMAN, MARV	PEREZ, GEORGE	$16.99/TP
4	9781401236884	JUN120239	TEEN TITANS VOL. 1: IT'S OUR RIGHT TO FIGHT (THE NEW 52)	LOBDELL, SCOTT	BOOTH, BRETT	$14.99/TP

DC COMICS SELECTED BACKLIST

SERIES # OR IMPRINT	ISBN	DIAMOND CODE	TITLE	AUTHOR	ARTIST	US$/ FORMAT
DC Comics	9781401235567	JUL120217	52 OMNIBUS	VARIOUS	VARIOUS	$150.00/HC
DC Comics	9781401237097	JUL120213	ALL STAR WESTERN VOL. 1: GUNS AND GOTHAM (THE NEW 52)	GRAY, JUSTIN & PALMIOTTI, JIMMY	MORITAT	$16.99/TP

SERIES # OR IMPRINT	ISBN	DIAMOND CODE	TITLE	AUTHOR	ARTIST	US$/ FORMAT
DC Comics	9781401235078	FEB120247	ANIMAL MAN VOL. 1: THE HUNT	LEMIRE, JEFF	FOREMAN, TRAVEL	$14.99/TP
DC Comics	9781401231132	MAR110349	AQUAMAN: DEATH OF THE PRINCE	VARIOUS	VARIOUS	$29.99/TP
DC Comics	9781401237103	FEB130206	AQUAMAN VOL. 1: THE TRENCH (THE NEW 52)	JOHNS, GEOFF	REIS, IVAN	$14.99/TP
DC Comics	9781401232627	APR110229	ASTRO CITY: LIFE IN THE BIG CITY	BUSIEK, KURT	ANDERSON, BRENT	$17.99/TP
DC Comics	9781401228245	SEP100247	BATGIRL: THE GREATEST STORIES EVER TOLD	VARIOUS	VARIOUS	$19.99/TP
DC Comics	9781401238148	NOV120261	BATGIRL VOL. 1: THE DARKEST REFLECTION	SIMONE, GAIL	SYAF, ARDIAN	$14.99/TP
DC Comics	9781401234768	APR120246	BATWING VOL. 1: THE LOST KINGDOM (THE NEW 52)	WINICK, JUDD	OLIVER, BEN	$14.99/TP
DC Comics	9781401231460	MAR110341	BATWOMAN: ELEGY	RUCKA, GREG	WILLIAMS III, J.H.	$17.99/TP
DC Comics	9781401237844	OCT120253	BATWOMAN VOL. 1: HYDROLOGY (THE NEW 52)	WILLIAMS III, J.H.	WILLIAMS III, J.H.	$14.99/TP
DC Comics	9781401231323	MAR120249	BIRDS OF PREY VOL. 1: END RUN	SIMONE, GAIL	BENES, ED	$14.99/TP
DC Comics	9781401234492	JUL120221	BIRDS OF PREY VOL. 2: DEATH OF ORACLE	SIMONE, GAIL	VARIOUS	$16.99/TP
DC Comics	9781401236991	JUN120236	BIRDS OF PREY VOL. 1: TROUBLE IN MIND (THE NEW 52)	SWIERCZYNSKI, DUANE	SAIZ, JESUS	$14.99/TP
DC Comics	9781401237141	AUG120247	BLACKHAWKS VOL. 1: THE GREAT LEAP FORWARD (THE NEW 52)	COSTA, MIKE	NOLAN, GRAHAM	$16.99/TP
DC Comics	9781401237134	AUG120246	BLUE BEETLE VOL. 1: METAMORPHOSIS (THE NEW 52)	BEDARD, TONY	GUARA, IG	$14.99/TP
DC Comics	9781401220068	FEB090201	BOOSTER GOLD: 52 PICK UP	JOHNS, GEOFF	JURGENS, DAN	$14.99/TP
DC Comics	9781401220143	SEP080164	BOOSTER GOLD: BLUE AND GOLD	JOHNS, GEOFF	JURGENS, DAN	$14.99/TP
DC Comics	9781401230241	JAN110325	BOOSTER GOLD: PAST IMPERFECT	GIFFEN, KEITH	OLLIFFE, PATRICK	$17.99/TP
DC Comics	9781401226435	JAN100297	BOOSTER GOLD : DAY OF DEATH	GIFFEN, KEITH	OLLIFFE, PATRICK	$14.99/TP
DC Comics	9781401222499	MAY090181	BOOSTER GOLD: REALITY LOST	JURGENS, DAN	JURGENS, DAN	$14.99/TP
DC Comics	9781401229184	SEP100248	BOOSTER GOLD: THE TOMORROW MEMORY	JURGENS, DAN	JURGENS, DAN	$17.99/TP
DC Comics	9781401237158	AUG120250	CAPTAIN ATOM VOL. 1: EVOLUTION (THE NEW 52)	KRUL, J.T.	WILLIAMS II, FREDDIE	$14.99/TP
DC Comics	9781401207175	MAY098043	CATWOMAN: WHEN IN ROME	LOEB, JEPH	SALE, TIM	$14.99/TP
DC Comics	9781401233846	OCT110246	CATWOMAN VOL. 1	BRUBAKER, ED	COOKE, DARWYN	$29.99/TP
DC Comics	9781401234645	FEB120248	CATWOMAN VOL. 1: THE GAME	WINICK, JUDD	MARCH, GUILLEM	$14.99/TP
DC Comics	9781401234744	FEB120263	CHALLENGERS OF THE UNKNOWN OMNIBUS BY JACK KIRBY	VARIOUS	KIRBY, JACK	$39.99/HC
DC Comics	9781401225919	OCT090244	THE CREEPER BY STEVE DITKO	VARIOUS	DITKO, STEVE	$39.99/HC
DC Comics	9781563898952	OCT098268	CRISIS ON MULTIPLE EARTHS VOL. 1	FOX, GARDNER	SEKOWSKY, MIKE	$14.99/TP
DC Comics	9781401200039	APR058270	CRISIS ON MULTIPLE EARTHS VOL. 2	FOX, GARDNER	SEKOWSKY, MIKE	$14.99/TP
DC Comics	9781401202316	MAY040298	CRISIS ON MULTIPLE EARTHS VOL. 3	FRIEDRICH, MIKE	SEKOWSKY, MIKE	$14.99/TP
DC Comics	9781401208575	FEB060261	CRISIS ON MULTIPLE EARTHS VOL. 4	VARIOUS	DILLIN, DICK	$14.99/TP
DC Comics	9781401207120	OCT068022	CRISIS ON INFINITE EARTHS	WOLFMAN, MARV	PÉREZ, GEORGE	$29.99/TP
DC Comics	9781401218178	JUN080241	DC UNIVERSE ILLUSTRATED BY NEAL ADAMS VOL. 1	VARIOUS	ADAMS, NEAL	$39.99/HC
DC Comics	9781401237165	AUG120251	DC UNIVERSE PRESENTS VOL. 1 FEATURING DEADMAN & CHALLENGERS OF THE UNKNOWN (THE NEW 52)	JENKINS, PAUL	CHANG, BERNARD	$16.99/TP
DC Comics	9781401226466	NOV090173	DC UNIVERSE: ORIGINS	VARIOUS	VARIOUS	$14.99/TP
DC Comics	9781401234041	JAN130303	DC UNIVERSE: SECRET ORIGINS	VARIOUS	VARIOUS	$24.99/TP
DC Comics	9781401233402	DEC120333	DC UNIVERSE BY ALAN MOORE	MOORE, ALAN	VARIOUS	$24.99/TP

DC COMICS SELECTED BACKLIST

SERIES # OR IMPRINT	ISBN	DIAMOND CODE	TITLE	AUTHOR	ARTIST	US$/ FORMAT
DC Comics	9781401231347	FEB120262	DC UNIVERSE: LEGACIES	WEIN, LEN	VARIOUS	$24.99/TP
DC Comics	9781401231163	FEB110188	DEADMAN VOL. 1	VARIOUS	ADAMS, NEAL	$19.99/TP
DC Comics	9781401233884	NOV110199	DEADMAN VOL. 2	VARIOUS	ADAMS, NEAL	$14.99/TP
DC Comics	9781401237288	SEP120236	DEADMAN VOL. 3	LEVITZ, PAUL	VARIOUS	$16.99/TP
DC Comics	9781401222116	MAY090185	DEATH OF THE NEW GODS	STARLIN, JIM	STARLIN, JIM	$19.99/TP
DC Comics	9781401234812	MAY120282	DEATHSTROKE VOL. 1: LEGACY (THE NEW 52)	HIGGINS, KYLE	BENNETT, JOE	$16.99/TP
DC Comics	9781401234720	APR120247	DEMON KNIGHTS VOL. 1: SEVEN AGAINST THE DARK	CORNELL, PAUL	NEVES, DIOGENES	$14.99/TP
DC Comics	9781401222826	MAR100239	FINAL CRISIS	MORRISON, GRANT	JONES, J.G.	$19.99/TP
DC Comics	9781401223250	JUL100195	FINAL CRISIS: LEGION OF 3 WORLDS	JOHNS, GEOFF	PEREZ, GEORGE	$14.99/TP
DC Comics	9781401223236	MAY100186	FINAL CRISIS: REVELATIONS	RUCKA, GREG	TAN, PHILIP	$14.99/TP
DC Comics	9781401231835	APR110202	FIRESTORM: THE NUCLEAR MAN	CONWAY, GERRY	MILGROM, AL	$17.99/TP
DC Comics	9781401237004	JUN120237	THE FURY OF FIRESTORM: THE NUCLEAR MEN VOL. 1: GOD PARTICLE (THE NEW 52)	SIMONE, GAIL	CINAR, YILDIRAY	$14.99/TP
DC Comics	9781401234713	MAR120244	FRANKENSTEIN, AGENT OF S.H.A.D.E. VOL. 1: WAR OF THE MONSTERS (THE NEW 52)	LEMIRE, JEFF	PONTICELLI, ALBERTO	$14.99/TP
DC Comics	9781401220372	DEC100248	GOTHAM CENTRAL BOOK 1: IN THE LINE OF DUTY	RUCKA, GREG	LARK, MICHAEL	$19.99/TP
DC Comics	9781401225438	APR110203	GOTHAM CENTRAL BOOK 2: JOKERS AND MADMEN	RUCKA, GREG	LARK, MICHAEL	$19.99/TP
DC Comics	9781401232320	JUL110257	GOTHAM CENTRAL BOOK 3: ON THE FREAK BEAT	RUCKA, GREG	LARK, MICHAEL	$19.99/TP
DC Comics	9781401231941	JAN120307	GOTHAM CENTRAL BOOK 4: CORRIGAN	RUCKA, GREG	KANO	$19.99/TP
DC Comics	9781401231385	MAR120250	GOTHAM CITY SIRENS: STRANGE FRUIT	BEDARD, TONY	GUINALDO, ANDRES	$14.99/TP
DC Comics	9781401234973	APR120248	GRIFTER VOL. 1: MOST WANTED	EDMONDSON, NATHAN	CAFU	$14.99/TP
DC Comics	9781401233976	NOV110200	HAWK & DOVE: GHOSTS & DEMONS	KESEL, KARL	LIEFELD, ROB	$14.99/TP
DC Comics	9781401234980	MAY120281	HAWK AND DOVE VOL. 1: FIRST STRIKES (THE NEW 52)	GATES, STERLING	LIEFELD, ROB	$16.99/TP
DC Comics	9781401232221	SEP110186	HAWKMAN OMNIBUS VOL. 1	JOHNS, GEOFF	MORALES, RAGS	$75.00/HC
DC Comics	9781563897986	FEB090206	HISTORY OF THE DC UNIVERSE	WOLFMAN, MARV	VARIOUS	$12.99/TP
DC Comics	9781563893148	MAR090185	HITMAN VOL. 1: A RAGE IN ARKHAM	ENNIS, GARTH	MCCREA, JOHN	$14.99/TP
DC Comics	9781401218423	NOV090172	HITMAN VOL. 2: TEN THOUSAND BULLETS	ENNIS, GARTH	MCCREA, JOHN	$17.99/TP
DC Comics	9781401228934	SEP100252	HITMAN VOL. 3: LOCAL HEROES	ENNIS, GARTH	MCCREA, JOHN	$17.99/TP
DC Comics	9781401230043	JAN110327	HITMAN VOL. 4: ACE OF KILLERS	ENNIS, GARTH	MCCREA, JOHN	$17.99/TP
DC Comics	9781401231187	SEP110183	HITMAN VOL. 5: TOMMY'S HEROES	ENNIS, GARTH	MCCREA, JOHN	$29.99/TP
DC Comics	9781401232825	JAN120309	HITMAN VOL. 6: FOR TOMORROW	ENNIS, GARTH	MCCREA, JOHN	$29.99/TP
DC Comics	9781401234003	MAY120294	HITMAN VOL. 7: CLOSING TIME	ENNIS, GARTH	MCCREA, JOHN	$29.99/TP
DC Comics	9781401237332	JUL120223	HUNTRESS: CROSSBOW AT THE CROSSROADS	LEVITZ, PAUL	TO, MARCUS	$14.99/TP
DC Comics	9781401233716	NOV110204	I, VAMPIRE	DEMATTEIS, MARK J.	SUTTON, THOMAS	$29.99/TP
DC Comics	9781401236878	JUL120212	I, VAMPIRE VOL. 1: TAINTED LOVE (THE NEW 52)	FIALKOV, JOSHUA HALE	SORRENTINO, ANDREA	$14.99/TP
DC Comics	9781401210601	FEB118148	INFINITE CRISIS	JOHNS, GEOFF	JIMENEZ, PHIL	$17.99/TP
DC Comics	9781401209223	JUL060154	INFINITE CRISIS COMPANION	RUCKA, GREG	VARIOUS	$14.99/TP
DC Comics	9781401235024	FEB120253	INFINITE CRISIS OMNIBUS	VARIOUS	VARIOUS	$150.00/HC

DC COMICS SELECTED BACKLIST

SERIES # OR IMPRINT	ISBN	DIAMOND CODE	TITLE	AUTHOR	ARTIST	US$/ FORMAT
DC Comics	9781401231057	FEB110201	INFINITY INC.: THE GENERATIONS SAGA VOL. 1	THOMAS, ROY	ORDWAY, JERRY	$39.99/HC
DC Comics	9781401232412	AUG110250	JACK KIRBY FOURTH WORLD OMNIBUS VOL. 1	KIRBY, JACK	KIRBY, JACK	$39.99/TP
DC Comics	9781401234409	JAN120310	JACK KIRBY FOURTH WORLD OMNIBUS VOL. 2	KIRBY, JACK	KIRBY, JACK	$29.99/TP
DC Comics	9781401235352	MAY120295	JACK KIRBY'S FOURTH WORLD OMNIBUS VOL. 3	KIRBY, JACK	KIRBY, JACK	$29.99/TP
DC Comics	9781401237462	SEP120240	JACK KIRBY'S 4TH WORLD OMNIBUS VOL. 4	KIRBY, JACK	KIRBY, JACK	$29.99/TP
DC Comics	9781401217907	JAN080186	JACK KIRBY'S O.M.A.C.	KIRBY, JACK	KIRBY, JACK	$24.99/TP
DC Comics	9781401218161	JUL080159	JACK KIRBY'S THE DEMON	KIRBY, JACK	KIRBY, JACK	$49.99/HC
DC Comics	9781401210953	JUN060192	JONAH HEX: FACE FULL OF VIOLENCE	GRAY, JUSTIN & PALMIOTTI, JIMMY	ROSS, LUKE	$12.99/TP
DC Comics	9781401227579	FEB100166	JONAH HEX: WELCOME TO PARADISE	ALBANO, JOHN	VARIOUS	$17.99/TP
DC Comics	9781401212490	JAN070305	JONAH HEX: GUNS OF VENGEANCE	GRAY, JUSTIN & PALMIOTTI, JIMMY	ROSS, LUKE	$12.99/TP
DC Comics	9781401214906	JUN098462	JONAH HEX: ORIGINS	GRAY, JUSTIN & PALMIOTTI, JIMMY	VARIOUS	$14.99/TP
DC Comics	9781401228996	JUL100196	JONAH HEX: COUNTING CORPSES	GRAY, JUSTIN & PALMIOTTI, JIMMY	VARIOUS	$14.99/TP
DC Comics	9781401230098	JAN110330	JONAH HEX: TALL TALES	GRAY, JUSTIN & PALMIOTTI, JIMMY	VARIOUS	$14.99/TP
DC Comics	9781401232489	AUG110248	JONAH HEX: BURY ME IN HELL	GRAY, JUSTIN & PALMIOTTI, JIMMY	VARIOUS	$17.99/TP
DC Comics	9781401225513	FEB110207	JONAH HEX: NO WAY BACK	GRAY, JUSTIN & PALMIOTTI, JIMMY	DEZUNIGA, TONY	$14.99/TP
DC Comics	9781401215415	MAY120270	THE JUDAS COIN	SIMONSON, WALTER	SIMONSON, WALTER	$22.99/HC
DC Comics	9781401236724	AUG120257	KAMANDI, THE LAST BOY ON EARTH OMNIBUS VOL. 2	KIRBY, JACK	KIRBY, JACK	$49.99/HC
DC Comics	9781401216696	JUN120247	LOBO: PORTRAIT OF A BASTICH	GIFFEN, KEITH AND GRANT, ALAN	BISLEY, SIMON	$19.99/TP
DC Comics	9781401234997	APR120249	MEN OF WAR VOL. 1: UNEASY COMPANY	BRANDON, IVAN	DERENICK, TOM	$19.99/TP
DC Comics	9781401237059	JUL120214	NIGHTWING VOL. 1: TRAPS AND TRAPEZES (THE NEW 52)	HIGGINS, KYLE	BARROWS, EDDY	$14.99/TP
DC Comics	9781401234829	MAY120263	O.M.A.C. VOL. 1: OMACTIVATE! (THE NEW 52)	DIDIO, DAN	GIFFEN, KEITH	$16.99/TP
DC Comics	9781401237325	JUN120249	PENGUIN: PAIN AND PREJUDICE	HURWITZ, GREGG	KUDRANSKI, SZYMON	$14.99/TP
DC Comics	9781563896484	FEB068129	PLANETARY VOL. 1: ALL OVER THE WORLD AND OTHER STORIES	ELLIS, WARREN	CASSADAY, JOHN	$14.99/TP
DC Comics	9781563897641	JAN068213	PLANETARY VOL. 2: THE FOURTH MAN	ELLIS, WARREN	CASSADAY, JOHN	$14.99/TP
DC Comics	9781401202941	JAN050354	PLANETARY VOL. 3: LEAVING THE 20TH CENTURY	ELLIS, WARREN	CASSADAY, JOHN	$14.99/TP
DC Comics	9781401223458	SEP100285	PLANETARY VOL. 4: SPACETIME ARCHEOLOGY	ELLIS, WARREN	CASSADAY, JOHN	$17.99/TP
DC Comics	9781401223465	MAR090211	RED	ELLIS, WARREN	HAMNER, CULLY	$14.99/TP
DC Comics	9781401231972	JAN110413	RED: BETTER RED THAN DEAD	VARIOUS	VARIOUS	$14.99/TP
DC Comics	9781401237127	AUG120248	RED HOOD AND THE OUTLAWS VOL. 1: REDEMPTION (THE NEW 52)	LOBDELL, SCOTT	ROCAFORT, KENNETH	$14.99/TP
DC Comics	9781401233631	OCT110247	RESURRECTION MAN VOL. 1	LANNING, ANDY	GUICE, BUTCH	$29.99/TP
DC Comics	9781401235261	MAY120284	RESURRECTION MAN VOL. 1: DEAD AGAIN (THE NEW 52)	LANNING, ANDY	DAGNINO, FERNANDO	$14.99/TP
DC Comics	9781401222994	APR090212	THE SANDMAN BY KIRBY AND SIMON	SIMON, JOE AND KIRBY, JACK	SIMON, JOE AND KIRBY, JACK	$39.99/HC
DC Comics	9781401237066	JUL120215	THE SAVAGE HAWKMAN VOL. 1: DARKNESS RISING (THE NEW 52)	DANIEL, TONY S.	TAN, PHILIP	$16.99/TP
DC Comics	9781401223274	MAY090184	SECRET SIX: UNHINGED	SIMONE, GAIL	SCOTT, NICOLA	$14.99/TP
DC Comics	9781401225985	JAN100302	SECRET SIX: DEPTHS	SIMONE, GAIL	SCOTT, NICOLA	$14.99/TP
DC Comics	9781401229047	JUL1002002	SECRET SIX: DANSE MACABRE	SIMONE, GAIL	CALAFIORE, JAMES	$14.99/TP

DC COMICS / VERTIGO SELECTED BACKLIST

IMPRINT	ISBN	DIAMOND CODE	TITLE	AUTHOR	ARTIST	US$/ FORMAT
DC Comics	9781401233624	OCT110254	SECRET SIX: THE DARKEST HOUSE	SIMONE, GAIL	CALAFIORE, JAMES	$16.99/TP
DC Comics	9781401231101	JAN120312	SECRET SOCIETY SUPER-VILLAINS	VARIOUS	VARIOUS	$24.99/HC
DC Comics	9781401231095	APR110209	SECRET SOCIETY SUPER-VILLAINS VOL. 2	LEVITZ, PAUL	VARIOUS	$39.99/HC
DC Comics	9781401228511	OCT110253	SEVEN SOLDIERS OF VICTORY BOOK 1	MORRISON, GRANT	VARIOUS	$29.99/TP
DC Comics	9781401229641	MAR120255	SEVEN SOLDIERS OF VICTORY BOOK 2	MORRISON, GRANT	VARIOUS	$29.99/TP
DC Comics	9781401212483	JAN070311	SGT ROCK: THE PROPHECY	KUBERT, JOE	KUBERT, JOE	$17.99/TP
DC Comics	9781401209742	DEC080160	SHAZAM! AND THE MONSTER SOCIETY OF EVIL	SMITH, JEFF	SMITH, JEFF	$19.99/TP
DC Comics	9781401216740	DEC070251	SHAZAM!: GREATEST STORIES EVER TOLD, VOL. 1	VARIOUS	VARIOUS	$24.99/TP
DC Comics	9781401234188	SEP110190	SPIRIT WORLD	KIRBY, JACK	KIRBY, JACK	$39.99/HC
DC Comics	9781401218376	FEB120268	THE STARMAN OMNIBUS VOL. 1	ROBINSON, JAMES	HARRIS, TONY	$29.99/TP
DC Comics	9781401221959	JUN120252	THE STARMAN OMNIBUS VOL. 2	ROBINSON, JAMES	HARRIS, TONY	$29.99/TP
DC Comics	9781401222840	FEB090214	THE STARMAN OMNIBUS VOL. 3	ROBINSON, JAMES	HARRIS, TONY	$49.99/HC
DC Comics	9781401225964	OCT090253	THE STARMAN OMNIBUS VOL. 4	ROBINSON, JAMES	HARRIS, TONY	$49.99/HC
DC Comics	9781401228897	JUN100209	THE STARMAN OMNIBUS VOL. 5	ROBINSON, JAMES	SNEJBJERG, PETER	$49.99/HC
DC Comics	9781401230449	SEP100254	THE STARMAN OMNIBUS VOL. 6	ROBINSON, JAMES	SNEJBJERG, PETER	$49.99/HC
DC Comics	9781401234843	MAR120245	STATIC SHOCK VOL. 1: SUPERCHARGED (THE NEW 52)	MCDANIEL, SCOTT	MCDANIEL, SCOTT	$16.99/TP
DC Comics	9781401231118	APR110208	THE STEVE DITKO OMNIBUS VOL. 1	VARIOUS	DITKO, STEVE	$59.99/HC
DC Comics	9781401232351	AUG110256	THE STEVE DITKO OMNIBUS VOL. 2	VARIOUS	DITKO, STEVE	$59.99/HC
DC Comics	9781401234201	OCT110250	STORMWATCH VOL. 1	ELLIS, WARREN	RANEY, TOM	$29.99/HC
DC Comics	9781401234836	FEB120251	STORMWATCH VOL. 1: DARK SIDE (THE NEW 52)	CORNELL, PAUL	SEPULVEDA, MIGUEL	$14.99/TP
DC Comics	9781401235444	APR120250	SUICIDE SQUAD VOL. 1: KICKED IN THE TEETH (THE NEW 52)	GLASS, ADAM	DALLOCCHIO, FEDERICO	$14.99/TP
DC Comics	9781401232511	SEP110188	SUPERBOY VOL. 1: SMALLVILLE ATTACKS	LEMIRE, JEFF	GALLO, PIER	$24.99/TP
DC Comics	9781401234850	MAY120285	SUPERBOY VOL. 1: INCUBATION (THE NEW 52)	LOBDELL, SCOTT	SILVA, R.B.	$14.99/TP
DC Comics	9781401227738	FEB110202	SUPERBOY: THE BOY OF STEEL	JOHNS, GEOFF	MANAPUL, FRANCIS	$14.99/TP
DC Comics	9781401236809	JUL120216	SUPERGIRL VOL. 1: LAST DAUGHTER OF KRYPTON (THE NEW 52)	GREEN, MICHAEL AND JOHNSON, MIKE	ASRAR, MAHMUD	$14.99/TP
DC Comics	9781401228095	MAY110253	TEAM-UPS OF THE BRAVE AND BOLD	STRACZYNSKI, J. MICHAEL	SAIZ, JESUS	$17.99/TP
DC Comics	9781401225360	MAY080220	TOM STRONG DELUXE VOL. 1	MOORE, ALAN	SPROUSE, CHRIS	$39.99/HC
DC Comics	9781401226800	DEC090253	TOM STRONG DELUXE VOL. 2	MOORE, ALAN	SPROUSE, CHRIS	$39.99/HC
DC Comics	9781401205737	JAN060370	TOP TEN: THE FORTY NINERS	MOORE, ALAN	HA, GENE	$17.99/TP
DC Comics	9781401235611	JUN120240	VOODOO VOL. 1: WHAT LIES BENEATH (THE NEW 52)	MARZ, RON	BASRI, SAMI	$14.99/TP
DC Comics	9780930289232	JUL088045	WATCHMEN	MOORE, ALAN	GIBBONS, DAVE	$19.99/TP
DC Comics	9781401227470	DEC090221	WEDNESDAY COMICS	VARIOUS	VARIOUS	$49.99/HC
DC Comics	9781401234775	MAY120298	WORLD'S FINEST	GIBBONS, DAVE	RUDE, STEVE	$17.99/TP
DC Comics	9781401202552	JUN100215	WORLD'S GREATEST SUPER-HEROES	DINI, PAUL	ROSS, ALEX	$29.99/TP
Vertigo	9781401221331	DEC080212	100%	POPE, PAUL	POPE, PAUL	$29.99/TP
Vertigo	9781401232016	MAR110342	100 BULLETS: THE DELUXE EDITION BOOK ONE	AZZARELLO, BRIAN	RISSO, EDUARDO	$49.99/HC

IMPRINT	ISBN	DIAMOND CODE	TITLE	AUTHOR	ARTIST	US$/FORMAT
Vertigo	9781401233723	DEC110322	100 BULLETS: THE DELUXE EDITION BOOK TWO	AZZARELLO, BRIAN	RISSO, EDUARDO	$49.99/HC
Vertigo	9781401237285	MAY120326	100 BULLETS: THE DELUXE EDITION BOOK THREE	AZZARELLO, BRIAN	RISSO, EDUARDO	$49.99/HC
Vertigo	9781563806453	JAN128095	100 BULLETS VOL. 1: FIRST SHOT, LAST CALL	AZZARELLO, BRIAN	RISSO, EDUARDO	$9.99/TP
Vertigo	9781563887115	JAN128189	100 BULLETS VOL. 2: SPLIT SECOND CHANCE	AZZARELLO, BRIAN	RISSO, EDUARDO	$14.99/TP
Vertigo	9781563888556	OCT098206	100 BULLETS VOL. 3: HANG UP ON THE HANG LOW	AZZARELLO, BRIAN	RISSO, EDUARDO	$14.99/TP
Vertigo	9781563889273	JUL098285	100 BULLETS VOL. 4: A FOREGONE TOMORROW	AZZARELLO, BRIAN	RISSO, EDUARDO	$19.99/TP
Vertigo	9781563889485	JUN108144	100 BULLETS VOL. 5: THE COUNTERFIFTH DETECTIVE	AZZARELLO, BRIAN	RISSO, EDUARDO	$14.99/TP
Vertigo	9781563889986	APR068251	100 BULLETS VOL. 6: SIX FEET UNDER THE GUN	AZZARELLO, BRIAN	RISSO, EDUARDO	$14.99/TP
Vertigo	9781401201890	DEC108150	100 BULLETS VOL. 7: SAMURAI	AZZARELLO, BRIAN	RISSO, EDUARDO	$14.99/TP
Vertigo	9781401204907	MAY050289	100 BULLETS VOL. 8: THE HARD WAY	AZZARELLO, BRIAN	RISSO, EDUARDO	$14.99/TP
Vertigo	9781401209285	JAN060374	100 BULLETS VOL. 9: STRYCHNINE LIVES	AZZARELLO, BRIAN	RISSO, EDUARDO	$14.99/TP
Vertigo	9781401208888	DEC118161	100 BULLETS VOL. 10: DECAYED	AZZARELLO, BRIAN	RISSO, EDUARDO	$14.99/TP
Vertigo	9781401213152	MAY070233	100 BULLETS VOL. 11: ONCE UPON A CRIME	AZZARELLO, BRIAN	RISSO, EDUARDO	$12.99/TP
Vertigo	9781401218398	JUN080292	100 BULLETS VOL. 12: DIRTY	AZZARELLO, BRIAN	RISSO, EDUARDO	$12.99/TP
Vertigo	9781401222871	APR090260	100 BULLETS VOL. 13: WILT	AZZARELLO, BRIAN	RISSO, EDUARDO	$19.99/TP
Vertigo	9781401230690	MAY110282	99 DAYS	CASALI, MATTEO	DONALDSON, KRISTIAN	$19.99/HC
Vertigo	9781401221478	AUG120281	A FLIGHT OF ANGELS	VARIOUS	GUAY, REBECCA	$17.99/TP
Vertigo	9781401232467	JUN110274	A GOD SOMEWHERE	ARCUDI, JOHN	SNEJBJERG, PETER	$17.99/TP
Vertigo	9781401231897	MAY110281	A HISTORY OF VIOLENCE	WAGNER, JOHN	LOCKE, VINCE	$14.99/TP
Vertigo	9781401210818	JUN100261	A SICKNESS IN THE FAMILY	MINA, DENISE	FUSO, ANTONIO	$19.99/HC
Vertigo	9781401223557	SEP110215	A.D.D.: ADOLESCENT DEMO DIVISION	RUSHKOFF, DOUGLAS	SUDZUKA, GORAN	$24.99/HC
Vertigo	9781401211868	DEC100289	AARON AND AHMED	CANTOR, JAY	ROMBERGER, JAMES	$24.99/TP
Vertigo	9781401221539	DEC060208	AIR VOL. 1: LETTERS FROM LOST COUNTRIES	WILSON, G. WILLOW	PERKER, M.K.	$9.99/TP
Vertigo	9781401224837	AUG090226	AIR VOL. 2: FLYING MACHINE	WILSON, G. WILLOW	PERKER, M.K.	$12.99/TP
Vertigo	9781401227067	FEB100248	AIR VOL. 3: PURELAND	WILSON, G. WILLOW	PERKER, M.K.	$14.99/TP
Vertigo	9781401228832	NOV100267	AIR VOL. 4: A HISTORY OF THE FUTURE	WILSON, G. WILLOW	PERKER, M.K.	$14.99/TP
Vertigo	9781401210571	JUN090256	THE ALCOHOLIC	AMES, JONATHAN	HASPIEL, DEAN	$14.99/TP
Vertigo	9781401212353	JAN070386	AMERICAN SPLENDOR VOL. 1: ANOTHER DAY	PEKAR, HARVEY	HASPIEL, DEAN	$14.99/TP
Vertigo	9781401221737	OCT080214	AMERICAN SPLENDOR VOL. 2: ANOTHER DOLLAR	PEKAR, HARVEY	LAPHAM, DAVID	$14.99/TP
Vertigo	9781401228740	JUL110284	AMERICAN VAMPIRE VOL. 1	KING, STEPHEN & SNYDER, SCOTT	ALBUQUERQUE, RAFAEL	$19.99/TP
Vertigo	9781401230708	FEB120269	AMERICAN VAMPIRE VOL. 2	SNYDER, SCOTT	ALBUQUERQUE, RAFAEL	$17.99/TP
Vertigo	9781401233341	JUN120280	AMERICAN VAMPIRE VOL. 3	SNYDER, SCOTT	ALBUQUERQUE, RAFAEL	$16.99/TP
Vertigo	9781401237189	MAY120322	AMERICAN VAMPIRE VOL. 4	SNYDER, SCOTT	ALBUQUERQUE, RAFAEL	$24.99/HC
Vertigo	9781563890055	OCT068037	ANIMAL MAN VOL. 1	MORRISON, GRANT	TRUOG, CHAS	$19.99/TP
Vertigo	9781563896907	JAN058098	ANIMAL MAN VOL. 2: ORIGIN OF THE SPECIES	MORRISON, GRANT	PUGH, STEVE	$19.99/TP
Vertigo	9781563889683	JAN068276	ANIMAL MAN VOL. 3: DEUS EX MACHINA	MORRISON, GRANT	TRUOG, CHAS	$19.99/TP

VERTIGO SELECTED BACKLIST

IMPRINT	ISBN	DIAMOND CODE	TITLE	AUTHOR	ARTIST	US$/ FORMAT
Vertigo	9781401226305	JAN110424	AREA 10	GAGE, CHRISTOS	SAMNEE, CHRIS	$12.99/TP
Vertigo	9781401232450	JUL110285	BAD DOING AND BIG IDEAS: A BILL WILLINGHAM DELUXE EDITION	WILLINGHAM, BILL	VARIOUS	$49.99/HC
Vertigo	9781401233358	DEC110318	BLACK ORCHID DELUXE EDITION	GAIMAN, NEIL	MCKEAN, DAVE	$24.99/HC
Vertigo	9781563890826	JAN078051	THE BOOKS OF MAGIC	GAIMAN, NEIL	BOLTON, JOHN	$19.99/HC
Vertigo	9781401226312	DEC100291	THE BRONX KILL	MILLIGAN, PETER	ROMBERGER, JAMES	$12.99/TP
Vertigo	9781401217341	JUN080290	CAIRO	WILSON, G. WILLOW	PERKER, M.K.	$17.99/TP
Vertigo	9781401225469	OCT100317	THE CHILL	STARR, JASON	BERTILORENZI, MICK	$12.99/TP
Vertigo	9781401227500	MAY100268	CINDERELLA: FROM FABLETOWN WITH LOVE	ROBERSON, CHRIS	MCMANUS, SHAWN	$14.99/TP
Vertigo	9781401233853	JAN120331	CINDERELLA: FABLES ARE FOREVER	ROBERSON, CHRIS	MCMANUS, SHAWN	$14.99/TP
Vertigo	9781563883438	STAR07350	COMPLETE MOONSHADOW	DEMATTEIS, J.M.	MUTH, JON J.	$39.95/TP
Vertigo	9781401215347	MAR110378	COWBOYS	PHILLIPS, GARY	HURTT, BRIAN	$19.99/TP
Vertigo	9781401222178	MAY100261	CUBA: MY REVOLUTION	INVERNA, LOCKPEZ	RASPIEL, DEAN	$24.99/TP
Vertigo	9781401224295	MAY100259	DARK ENTRIES	RANKIN, IAN	DELL'EDERA, WERTHER	$12.99/TP
Vertigo	9781401221614	MAY110284	DARK RAIN: A NEW ORLEANS STORY	JOHNSON, MAT	GANE, SIMON	$19.99/TP
Vertigo	9781401228696	NOV100268	DAYTRIPPER	BA, GABRIEL	MOON, FABIO	$19.99/TP
Vertigo	9781401234805	FEB120290	DEADENDERS	BRUBAKER, ED	BOND, PHILIP J.	$29.99/TP
Vertigo	9781401235482	JUN120272	DEATH DELUXE EDITION	GAIMAN, NEIL	BACHALO, CHRIS	$29.99/HC
Vertigo	9781563899386	FEB078187	DEATH: AT DEATH'S DOOR	THOMPSON, JILL	THOMPSON, JILL	$9.99/TP
Vertigo	9781563891335	JUL058228	DEATH: THE HIGH COST OF LIVING	GAIMAN, NEIL	BACHALO, CHRIS	$12.99/TP
Vertigo	9781401224776	NOV100264	DELIRIUM'S PARTY: A LITTLE ENDLESS STORY BOOK	THOMPSON, JILL	THOMPSON, JILL	$14.99/HC
Vertigo	9781401216214	MAR108116	DEMO	WOOD, BRIAN	CLOONAN, BECKY	$24.99/TP
Vertigo	9781401229955	DEC100292	DEMO VOL. 2	WOOD, BRIAN	CLOONAN, BECKY	$17.99/TP
Vertigo	9781401210625	OCT118125	DMZ VOL. 1: ON THE GROUND	WOOD, BRIAN	BURCHIELLI, RICCARDO	$12.99/TP
Vertigo	9781401212476	NOV060292	DMZ VOL. 2: BODY OF A JOURNALIST	WOOD, BRIAN	BURCHIELLI, RICCARDO	$12.99/TP
Vertigo	9781401214760	JUN070267	DMZ VOL. 3: PUBLIC WORKS	WOOD, BRIAN	BURCHIELLI, RICCARDO	$12.99/TP
Vertigo	9781401216627	DEC070294	DMZ VOL. 4: FRIENDLY FIRE	WOOD, BRIAN	BURCHIELLI, RICCARDO	$12.99/TP
Vertigo	9781401218331	JUL108009	DMZ VOL. 5: THE HIDDEN WAR	WOOD, BRIAN	BURCHIELLI, RICCARDO	$14.99/TP
Vertigo	9781401221300	NOV080228	DMZ VOL. 6: BLOOD IN THE GAME	WOOD, BRIAN	BURCHIELLI, RICCARDO	$12.99/TP
Vertigo	9781401224301	JUN090262	DMZ VOL. 7: WAR POWERS	WOOD, BRIAN	BURCHIELLI, RICCARDO	$14.99/TP
Vertigo	9781401227265	APR100271	DMZ VOL. 8: HEARTS AND MINDS	WOOD, BRIAN	BURCHIELLI, RICCARDO	$16.99/TP
Vertigo	9781401228962	NOV100272	DMZ VOL. 9: M.I.A.	WOOD, BRIAN	BURCHIELLI, RICCARDO	$14.99/TP
Vertigo	9781401231507	FEB110260	DMZ VOL. 10: COLLECTIVE PUNISHMENT	WOOD, BRIAN	BURCHIELLI, RICCARDO	$14.99/TP
Vertigo	9781401233891	DEC110321	DMZ VOL. 11: FREE STATES RISING	WOOD, BRIAN	BURCHIELLI, RICCARDO	$19.99/TP
Vertigo	9781401234799	MAR120276	DMZ VOL. 12: FIVE NATIONS OF NEW YORK	WOOD, BRIAN	BURCHIELLI, RICCARDO	$14.99/TP
Vertigo	9781401237424	SEP120264	DOMINIQUE LAVEAU, VOODOO CHILD VOL. 1: REQUIEM	HINDS, SELWYN SEYFU	COWAN, DENYS	$14.99/TP
Vertigo	9781401229481	FEB110213	DONG XOAI VIETNAM 1965	KUBERT, JOE	KUBERT, JOE	$19.99/TP

IMPRINT	ISBN	DIAMOND CODE	TITLE	AUTHOR	ARTIST	US$/ FORMAT
Vertigo	9781563890345	JAN058100	DOOM PATROL VOL. 1: CRAWLING FROM THE WRECKAGE	MORRISON, GRANT	CASE, RICHARD	$19.99/TP
Vertigo	9781401203429	JUL058223	DOOM PATROL VOL. 2: THE PAINTING THAT ATE PARIS	MORRISON, GRANT	CASE, RICHARD	$19.99/TP
Vertigo	9781401207267	AUG050282	DOOM PATROL VOL. 3: DOWN PARADISE WAY	MORRISON, GRANT	CASE, RICHARD	$19.99/TP
Vertigo	9781401209995	OCT060288	DOOM PATROL VOL. 4: MUSCLEBOUND	MORRISON, GRANT	CASE, RICHARD	$19.99/TP
Vertigo	9781401212025	OCT060288	DOOM PATROL VOL. 5: MAGIC BUS	MORRISON, GRANT	CASE, RICHARD	$19.99/TP
Vertigo	9781401218245	OCT070251	DOOM PATROL VOL. 6: PLANET LOVE	MORRISON, GRANT	CASE, RICHARD	$19.99/TP
Vertigo	9781401228217	FEB110253	THE EXECUTOR	EVANS, JON	MUTTI, ANDREA	$12.99/TP
Vertigo	9781401210649	MAY060233	THE EXTERMINATORS VOL. 1: BUG BROTHERS	OLIVER, SIMON	MOORE, TONY	$9.99/TP
Vertigo	9781401212216	DEC060297	THE EXTERMINATORS VOL. 2: INSURGENCY	OLIVER, SIMON	MOORE, TONY	$12.99/TP
Vertigo	9781401214753	JUL070298	THE EXTERMINATORS VOL. 3: LIES OF OUR FATHERS	OLIVER, SIMON	MOORE, TONY	$14.99/TP
Vertigo	9781401216856	JAN080250	THE EXTERMINATORS VOL. 4: CROSSFIRE AND COLLATERAL	OLIVER, SIMON	MOORE, TONY	$14.99/TP
Vertigo	9781401219703	AUG080225	THE EXTERMINATORS VOL. 5: BUG BROTHERS FOREVER	OLIVER, SIMON	MOORE, TONY	$14.99/TP
Vertigo	9781401237554	FEB120285	FABLES VOL. 1: LEGENDS IN EXILE	WILLINGHAM, BILL	MEDINA, LAN	$12.99/TP
Vertigo	9781401200770	MAR058123	FABLES VOL. 2: ANIMAL FARM	WILLINGHAM, BILL	BUCKINGHAM, MARK	$12.99/TP
Vertigo	9781401202569	JAN128247	FABLES VOL. 3: STORYBOOK LOVE	WILLINGHAM, BILL	BUCKINGHAM, MARK	$14.99/TP
Vertigo	9781401202224	OCT058021	FABLES VOL. 4: MARCH OF THE WOODEN SOLDIERS	WILLINGHAM, BILL	BUCKINGHAM, MARK	$17.99/TP
Vertigo	9781401204860	JAN050373	FABLES VOL. 5: THE MEAN SEASONS	WILLINGHAM, BILL	BUCKINGHAM, MARK	$14.99/TP
Vertigo	9781401205003	OCT050317	FABLES VOL. 6: HOMELANDS	WILLINGHAM, BILL	BUCKINGHAM, MARK	$14.99/TP
Vertigo	9781401210007	MAR060384	FABLES VOL. 7: ARABIAN NIGHTS (AND DAYS)	WILLINGHAM, BILL	BUCKINGHAM, MARK	$14.99/TP
Vertigo	9781401210014	SEP060313	FABLES VOL. 8: WOLVES	WILLINGHAM, BILL	BUCKINGHAM, MARK	$17.99/TP
Vertigo	9781401213169	MAR070271	FABLES VOL. 9: SONS OF EMPIRE	WILLINGHAM, BILL	BUCKINGHAM, MARK	$17.99/TP
Vertigo	9781401216863	FEB080297	FABLES VOL. 10: THE GOOD PRINCE	WILLINGHAM, BILL	BUCKINGHAM, MARK	$17.99/TP
Vertigo	9781401218130	AUG080228	FABLES VOL. 11: WAR AND PIECES	BUCKINGHAM, MARK	BUCKINGHAM, MARK	$17.99/TP
Vertigo	9781401223168	MAY090238	FABLES VOL. 12: THE DARK AGES	WILLINGHAM, BILL	BUCKINGHAM, MARK	$17.99/TP
Vertigo	9781401225728	NOV090228	FABLES VOL. 13: THE GREAT FABLES CROSSOVER	WILLINGHAM, BILL	BUCKINGHAM, MARK	$17.99/TP
Vertigo	9781401228804	SEP100304	FABLES VOL. 14: WITCHES	WILLINGHAM, BILL	BUCKINGHAM, MARK	$17.99/TP
Vertigo	9781401230005	JAN110422	FABLES VOL. 15: ROSE RED	WILLINGHAM, BILL	BUCKINGHAM, MARK	$17.99/TP
Vertigo	9781401233066	SEP110221	FABLES VOL. 16: SUPER TEAM	WILLINGHAM, BILL	BUCKINGHAM, MARK	$14.99/TP
Vertigo	9781401235161	APR120282	FABLES VOL. 17: INHERIT THE WIND	WILLINGHAM, BILL	BUCKINGHAM, MARK	$14.99/TP
Vertigo	9781401224790	JUL120247	FABLES: WEREWOLVES OF THE HEARTLAND	WILLINGHAM, BILL	FERN, JIM	$22.99/TP
Vertigo	9781401203606	DEC070297	FABLES: 1001 NIGHTS OF SNOWFALL	WILLINGHAM, BILL	VARIOUS	$14.99/TP
Vertigo	9781401224271	MAY090235	FABLES DELUXE EDITION BOOK ONE	WILLINGHAM, BILL	BUCKINGHAM, MARK	$29.99/HC
Vertigo	9781401228798	JUL100251	FABLES DELUXE EDITION BOOK TWO	WILLINGHAM, BILL	BUCKINGHAM, MARK	$29.99/HC
Vertigo	9781401230875	APR110244	FABLES DELUXE EDITION BOOK THREE	WILLINGHAM, BILL	BUCKINGHAM, MARK	$29.99/HC
Vertigo	9781401233907	OCT110292	FABLES DELUXE EDITION BOOK FOUR	WILLINGHAM, BILL	BUCKINGHAM, MARK	$29.99/HC
Vertigo	9781401234866	JAN120330	FABLES DELUXE EDITION BOOK FIVE	WILLINGHAM, BILL	BUCKINGHAM, MARK	$29.99/HC

VERTIGO SELECTED BACKLIST

IMPRINT	ISBN	DIAMOND CODE	TITLE	AUTHOR	ARTIST	US$/FORMAT
Vertigo	9781401237240	OCT120295	FABLES DELUXE EDITION BOOK SIX	WILLINGHAM, BILL	BUCKINGHAM, MARK	$29.99/HC
Vertigo	9781401235505	AUG120283	FAIREST VOL. 1: WIDE AWAKE	WILLINGHAM, BILL	JIMENEZ, PHIL	$14.99/TP
Vertigo	9781401216634	DEC070292	FAKER	CAREY, MIKE	JOCK	$14.99/TP
Vertigo	9781401200138	APR128207	THE FILTH	MORRISON, GRANT	WESTON, CHRIS	$19.99/TP
Vertigo	9781401211851	MAY100260	FILTHY RICH	AZZARELLO, BRIAN	SANTOS, VICTOR	$12.99/TP
Vertigo	9781401232214	OCT110285	FLEX MENTALLO: MAN OF MUSCLE MYSTERY DELUXE EDITION	MORRISON, GRANT	QUITELY, FRANK	$22.99/HC
Vertigo	9781401229504	MAY110283	FOGTOWN	GABRYCH, ANDERSEN	RADER, BRAD	$12.99/TP
Vertigo	9781401200589	AUG060290	THE FOUNTAIN	ARONOFSKY, DARREN	WILLIAMS, KENT	$18.99/TP
Vertigo	9781401228279	FEB120281	GET JIRO!	BOURDAIN, ANTHONY AND ROSE, JOEL	FOSS, LANGDON	$24.99/TP
Vertigo	9781401235574	JUL120243	THE GIRL WITH THE DRAGON TATTOO BOOK 1	MINA, DENISE	MANCO, LEONARDO & MUTTI, ANDREA	$19.99/TP
Vertigo	9781401203047	JAN080244	GOD SAVE THE QUEEN	CAREY, MIKE	BOLTON, JOHN	$12.99/TP
Vertigo	9781401223519	NOV110226	GONE TO AMERIKAY	MCCULLOUGH, DEREK	DORAN, COLLEEN	$24.99/TP
Vertigo	9781401226985	FEB100245	NEIL YOUNG'S GREENDALE	DYSART, JOSH	CHIANG, CLIFF	$19.99/HC
Vertigo	9781401211011	JUL110291	THE GREEN WOMAN	STRAUB, PETER	BOLTON, JOHN	$17.99/TP
Vertigo	9781401220075	JUL090286	HEAVY LIQUID	POPE, PAUL	POPE, PAUL	$24.99/TP
Vertigo	9781401220792	MAR108095	HOUSE OF MYSTERY VOL. 1: ROOM AND BOREDOM	WILLINGHAM, BILL	ROSSI, LUCA	$14.99/TP
Vertigo	9781401222765	MAR090236	HOUSE OF MYSTERY VOL. 2: LOVE STORIES FOR DEAD PEOPLE	STURGES, MATTHEW	ROSSI, LUCA	$14.99/TP
Vertigo	9781401225810	OCT090303	HOUSE OF MYSTERY VOL. 3: THE SPACE BETWEEN	STURGES, MATTHEW	ROSSI, LUCA	$14.99/TP
Vertigo	9781401227562	APR100281	HOUSE OF MYSTERY VOL. 4: THE BEAUTY OF DECAY	STURGES, MATTHEW	ROSSI, LUCA	$17.99/TP
Vertigo	9781401229818	OCT100325	HOUSE OF MYSTERY VOL. 5: UNDER NEW MANAGEMENT	STURGES, MATTHEW	ROSSI, LUCA	$14.99/TP
Vertigo	9781401231545	FEB110258	HOUSE OF MYSTERY VOL. 6: SAFE AS HOUSES	STURGES, MATTHEW	ROSSI, LUCA	$14.99/TP
Vertigo	9781401232641	SEP110224	HOUSE OF MYSTERY VOL. 7: CONCEPTION	STURGES, MATTHEW	ROSSI, LUCA	$14.99/TP
Vertigo	9781401234959	MAY120324	HOUSE OF MYSTERY VOL. 8: DESOLATION	STURGES, MATTHEW	ROSSI, LUCA	$14.99/TP
Vertigo	9781401222345	JUN110354	HOW UNDERSTAND ISRAEL IN 60 DAYS OR LESS	GLIDDEN, SARAH	GLIDDEN, SARAH	$19.99/TP
Vertigo	9781401226664	OCT090298	HUMAN TARGET	MILLIGAN, PETER	BRUKOVIC, EDVIN	$14.99/TP
Vertigo	9781401230616	NOV100270	HUMAN TARGET: SECOND CHANCES	MILLIGAN, PETER	PULIDO, JAVIER	$19.99/TP
Vertigo	9781401210884	FEB090259	INCOGNEGRO	JOHNSON, MAT	PLEECE, WARREN	$14.99/TP
Vertigo	9781401234591	APR120288	THE INVISIBLES OMNIBUS	GRANT MORRISON	VARIOUS	$150.00/HC
Vertigo	9781563882677	SEP068118	THE INVISIBLES: SAY YOU WANT A REVOLUTION VOL. 1	MORRISON, GRANT	YEOWELL, STEVE	$19.99/TP
Vertigo	9781563887023	OCT058208	THE INVISIBLES: APOCALIPSTICK VOL. 2	MORRISON, GRANT	THOMPSON, JILL	$19.99/TP
Vertigo	9781563897283	JUN058158	THE INVISIBLES: ENTROPY IN THE U.K. VOL. 3	MORRISON, GRANT	JIMENEZ, PHIL	$19.99/TP
Vertigo	9781563894442	DEC118104	THE INVISIBLES: BLOODY HELL IN AMERICA VOL. 4	MORRISON, GRANT	JIMENEZ, PHIL	$12.99/TP
Vertigo	9781563894893	AUG058062	THE INVISIBLES: COUNTING DOWN TO NONE VOL. 5	MORRISON, GRANT	JIMENEZ, PHIL	$19.99/TP
Vertigo	9781563896002	FEB068163	THE INVISIBLES: KISSING MR. QUIMPER VOL. 6	MORRISON, GRANT	WESTON, CHRIS	$19.99/TP
Vertigo	9781401200190	JAN078237	THE INVISIBLES: THE INVISIBLE KINGDOM VOL. 7	MORRISON, GRANT	BOND, PHILIP J.	$19.99/TP
Vertigo	9781401228658	DEC100299	IZOMBIE VOL. 1: DEAD TO THE WORLD	ROBERSON, CHRIS	ALLRED, MIKE	$14.99/TP

VERTIGO SELECTED BACKLIST

IMPRINT	ISBN	DIAMOND CODE	TITLE	AUTHOR	ARTIST	US$/ FORMAT
Vertigo	9781401232962	JUN110353	IZOMBIE VOL. 2: UVAMPIRE	ROBERSON, CHRIS	ALLRED, MIKE	$14.99/TP
Vertigo	9781401233709	NOV110232	IZOMBIE VOL. 3: SIX FEET UNDER AND RISING	ROBERSON, CHRIS	ALLRED, MIKE	$14.99/TP
Vertigo	9781401236877	SEP120261	IZOMBIE VOL. 4: REPOSSESSED	ROBERSON, CHRIS	ALLRED, MIKE	$16.99/TP
Vertigo	9781401212223	NOV060300	JACK OF FABLES VOL. 1: THE (NEARLY) GREAT ESCAPE	STURGES, MATTHEW & WILLINGHAM, BILL	AKINS, TONY	$14.99/TP
Vertigo	9781401214555	JUL070305	JACK OF FABLES VOL. 2: JACK OF HEARTS	STURGES, MATTHEW & WILLINGHAM, BILL	AKINS, TONY	$14.99/TP
Vertigo	9781401218546	MAR080229	JACK OF FABLES VOL. 3: THE BAD PRINCE	STURGES, MATTHEW & WILLINGHAM, BILL	AKINS, TONY	$14.99/TP
Vertigo	9781401218796	SEP080219	JACK OF FABLES VOL. 4: AMERICANA	STURGES, MATTHEW & WILLINGHAM, BILL	AKINS, TONY	$14.99/TP
Vertigo	9781401221386	DEC080210	JACK OF FABLES VOL. 5: TURNING PAGES	STURGES, MATTHEW & WILLINGHAM, BILL	AKINS, TONY	$14.99/TP
Vertigo	9781401225001	JUL090281	JACK OF FABLES VOL. 6: THE BIG BOOK OF WAR	STURGES, MATTHEW & WILLINGHAM, BILL	AKINS, TONY	$14.99/TP
Vertigo	9781401227128	MAR100298	JACK OF FABLES VOL. 7: THE NEW ADVENTURES OF JACK AND JACK	STURGES, MATTHEW & WILLINGHAM, BILL	AKINS, TONY	$14.99/TP
Vertigo	9781401229825	OCT100327	JACK OF FABLES VOL. 8: THE FULMINATE BLADE	STURGES, MATTHEW & WILLINGHAM, BILL	AKINS, TONY	$14.99/TP
Vertigo	9781401231552	APR110245	JACK OF FABLES VOL. 9: THE END	STURGES, MATTHEW & WILLINGHAM, BILL	AKINS, TONY	$17.99/TP
Vertigo	9781401231798	FEB110214	JEW GANGSTER	KUBERT, JOE	KUBERT, JOE	$14.99/TP
Vertigo	9781401237479		JOE THE BARBARIAN	MORRISON, GRANT	MURPHY, SEAN	$19.99/TP
Vertigo	9781401230067	DEC100302	JOHN CONSTANTINE, HELLBLAZER VOL. 1: ORIGINAL SINS	DELANO, JAMIE	RIDGWAY, JOHN	$19.99/TP
Vertigo	9781401233020	SEP110216	JOHN CONSTANTINE, HELLBLAZER VOL. 2: THE DEVIL YOU KNOW	DELANO, JAIME	LLOYD, DAVID	$19.99/TP
Vertigo	9781401235192	MAR120279	JOHN CONSTANTINE, HELLBLAZER VOL. 3: THE FEAR MACHINE	DELANO, JAMIE	MCKEAN, DAVE	$24.99/TP
Vertigo	9781401236908	AUG120288	JOHN CONSTANTINE, HELLBLAZER VOL. 4: THE FAMILY MAN	VARIOUS	LLOYD, DAVID	$18.99/TP
Vertigo	9781563898713	STAR18495	JOHN CONSTANTINE, HELLBLAZER: FREEZES OVER	AZZARELLO, BRIAN	BRADSTREET, TIM	$14.95/TP
Vertigo	9781401210038	JAN060378	JOHN CONSTANTINE, HELLBLAZER: PAPA MIDNITE	JOHNSON, MAT	AKINS, TONY	$12.99/TP
Vertigo	9781401214531	JUN070273	JOHN CONSTANTINE, HELLBLAZER: THE GIFT	CAREY, MIKE	MANCO, LEONARDO	$14.99/TP
Vertigo	9781401204853	MAR060480	JOHN CONSTANTINE, HELLBLAZER: RED SEPULCHRE	CAREY, MIKE	DILLON, STEVE	$12.99/TP
Vertigo	9781401203177	APR060290	JOHN CONSTANTINE, HELLBLAZER: ALL HIS ENGINES	CAREY, MIKE	MANCO, LEONARDO	$14.99/TP
Vertigo	9781401210021	MAY060237	JOHN CONSTANTINE, HELLBLAZER: STATIONS OF THE CROSS	CAREY, MIKE	BRADSTREET, TIM	$14.99/TP
Vertigo	9781401216511	NOV070287	JOHN CONSTANTINE, HELLBLAZER: JOYRIDE	DIGGLE, ANDY	MANCO, LEONARDO	$14.99/TP
Vertigo	9781401220396	NOV100274	JOHN CONSTANTINE, HELLBLAZER: PANDEMONIUM	DELANO, JAMIE	JOCK	$17.99/TP
Vertigo	9781401231538	FEB110256	JOHN CONSTANTINE, HELLBLAZER: CITY OF DEMONS	SPENCER, SI	MURPHY, SEAN	$14.99/TP
Vertigo	9781401225018	AUG090230	JOHN CONSTANTINE, HELLBLAZER: SCAB	MILLIGAN, PETER	CAMMUNCOLI, GIUSEPPE	$14.99/TP
Vertigo	9781401227289	MAR100308	JOHN CONSTANTINE, HELLBLAZER: HOOKED	MILLIGAN, PETER	CAMMUNCOLI, GIUSEPPE	$14.99/TP
Vertigo	9781401228484	JUL100252	JOHN CONSTANTINE, HELLBLAZER: INDIA	MILLIGAN, PETER	CAMMUNCOLI, GIUSEPPE	$14.99/TP
Vertigo	9781401231521	APR110249	JOHN CONSTANTINE, HELLBLAZER: BLOODY CARNATIONS	MILLIGAN, PETER	CAMMUNCOLI, GIUSEPPE	$16.99/TP
Vertigo	9781401233990	NOV110228	JOHN CONSTANTINE, HELLBLAZER: PHANTOM PAINS	MILLIGAN, PETER	CAMMUNCOLI, GIUSEPPE	$14.99/TP
Vertigo	9781401237202	JUL120255	JOHN CONSTANTINE, HELLBLAZER: THE DEVIL'S TRENCHCOAT	MILLIGAN, PETER	CAMMUNCOLI, GIUSEPPE	$16.99/TP
Vertigo	9781401204280	NOV100265	THE LITTLE ENDLESS STORYBOOK	THOMPSON, JILL	THOMPSON, JILL	$14.99/HC
Vertigo	9781401227333	NOV090232	THE LOSERS BOOK ONE	DIGGLE, ANDY	JOCK	$19.99/TP
Vertigo	9781401229238	MAY100275	THE LOSERS BOOK TWO	DIGGLE, ANDY	JOCK	$24.99/TP

VERTIGO SELECTED BACKLIST

IMPRINT	ISBN	DIAMOND CODE	TITLE	AUTHOR	ARTIST	US$/FORMAT
Vertigo	9781401222918	APR090268	MADAME XANADU VOL. 1: DISENCHANTED	WAGNER, MATT	REEDER, AMY	$12.99/TP
Vertigo	9781401226244	NOV090237	MADAME XANADU VOL. 2: EXODUS NOIR	WAGNER, MATT	KALUTA, MICHAEL W.M.	$12.99/TP
Vertigo	9781401228811	OCT100331	MADAME XANADU VOL. 3: BROKEN HOUSE OF CARDS	WAGNER, MATT	REEDER, AMY	$17.99/TP
Vertigo	9781401231590	MAY110295	MADAME XANADU VOL. 4: EXTRA SENSORY	WAGNER, MATT	REEDER, AMY	$17.99/TP
Vertigo	9781401229597	JUL110278	MARZI	SOWA, MARZENA	SAVOIA, SYLVAIN	$17.99/TP
Vertigo	9781563892462	SEP058283	MR. PUNCH	GAIMAN, NEIL	MCKEAN, DAVE	$18.99/TP
Vertigo	9781563891892	STAR18959	MYSTERY PLAY	MORRISON, GRANT	MUTH, JON J.	$12.95/TP
Vertigo	9781401234577	MAR120280	NEIL GAIMAN'S MIDNIGHT DAYS DELUXE EDITION	GAIMAN, NEIL	MCKEAN, DAVE	$24.99/HC
Vertigo	9781401210076	NOV060304	NEIL GAIMAN'S NEVERWHERE	CAREY, MIKE	FABRY, GLENN	$18.99/TP
Vertigo	9781401211547	APR080265	THE NEW YORK FOUR	WOOD, BRIAN	KELLY, RYAN	$9.99/TP
Vertigo	9781401232917	JUN110351	THE NEW YORK FIVE	WOOD, BRIAN	KELLY, RYAN	$14.99/TP
Vertigo	9781401219185	AUG118083	NORTHLANDERS VOL. 1: SVEN THE RETURNED	WOOD, BRIAN	GIANFELICE, DAVIDE	$14.99/TP
Vertigo	9781401222963	APR090272	NORTHLANDERS VOL. 2: THE CROSS AND THE HAMMER	WOOD, BRIAN	KELLY, RYAN	$14.99/TP
Vertigo	9781401226206	JUL118131	NORTHLANDERS VOL. 3: BLOOD IN THE SNOW	WOOD, BRIAN	LOLOS, VASILIS	$16.99/TP
Vertigo	9781401228507	JUL100258	NORTHLANDERS VOL. 4: THE PLAGUE WIDOW	WOOD, BRIAN	FERNANDEZ, LEANDRO	$16.99/TP
Vertigo	9781401231606	APR110247	NORTHLANDERS VOL. 5: METAL	WOOD, BRIAN	BURCHIELLI, RICCARDO	$17.99/TP
Vertigo	9781401233662	DEC110323	NORTHLANDERS VOL. 6: THOR'S DAUGHTER	WOOD, BRIAN	GANE, SIMON	$14.99/TP
Vertigo	9781401236915	SEP120265	NORTHLANDERS VOL. 7: THE ICELANDIC TRILOGY	WOOD, BRIAN	VARIOUS	$16.99/TP
Vertigo	9781401202682	JUL088085	ORBITER	ELLIS, WARREN	DORAN, COLLEEN	$17.99/TP
Vertigo	9781401203566	AUG050289	THE ORIGINALS	GIBBONS, DAVE	GIBBONS, DAVE	$17.99/TP
Vertigo	9781401219024	DEC090263	OTHER LIVES	BAGGE, PETER	BAGGE, PETER	$24.99/TP
Vertigo	9781401213503	FEB070359	THE OTHER SIDE	AARON, JASON	STEWART, CAMERON	$12.99/TP
Vertigo	9781401215354	OCT100316	NOCHE ROJA	OLIVER, SIMON	LATOUR, JASON	$19.99/HC
Vertigo	9781401225377	SEP100303	PETER & MAX: A FABLES NOVEL	WILLINGHAM, BILL	LEIALOHA, STEVE	$14.99/TP
Vertigo	9781401222796	FEB090260	PREACHER BOOK ONE	ENNIS, GARTH	DILLON, STEVE	$39.99/HC
Vertigo	9781401225797	OCT090299	PREACHER BOOK TWO	ENNIS, GARTH	DILLON, STEVE	$39.99/HC
Vertigo	9781401230166	AUG100271	PREACHER BOOK THREE	ENNIS, GARTH	DILLON, STEVE	$39.99/HC
Vertigo	9781401232504		PREACHER BOOK FIVE	ENNIS, GARTH	DILLON, STEVE	$39.99/HC
Vertigo	9781401234157	SEP110226	PREACHER BOOK SIX	ENNIS, GARTH	DILLON, STEVE	$39.99/HC
Vertigo	9781563892615	JUL108037	PREACHER VOL. 1: GONE TO TEXAS	ENNIS, GARTH	DILLON, STEVE	$17.99/TP
Vertigo	9781563893124	JUL118011	PREACHER VOL. 2: UNTIL THE END OF THE WORLD	ENNIS, GARTH	DILLON, STEVE	$17.99/TP
Vertigo	9781563893278	JUL066334	PREACHER VOL. 3: PROUD AMERICANS	ENNIS, GARTH	DILLON, STEVE	$14.99/TP
Vertigo	9781563894053	FEB118118	PREACHER VOL. 4: ANCIENT HISTORY	ENNIS, GARTH	DILLON, STEVE	$17.99/TP
Vertigo	9781563894282	JUL128119	PREACHER VOL. 5: DIXIE FRIED	ENNIS, GARTH	DILLON, STEVE	$14.99/TP
Vertigo	9781563894909	MAY050301	PREACHER VOL. 6: WAR IN THE SUN	ENNIS, GARTH	DILLON, STEVE	$17.99/TP
Vertigo	9781563895197	MAY050300	PREACHER VOL. 7: SALVATION	ENNIS, GARTH	DILLON, STEVE	$17.99/TP

VERTIGO SELECTED BACKLIST

IMPRINT	ISBN	DIAMOND CODE	TITLE	AUTHOR	ARTIST	US$/FORMAT
Vertigo	9781563896170	SEP058101	PREACHER VOL. 8: ALL HELL'S A-COMING	ENNIS, GARTH	DILLON, STEVE	$17.99/TP
Vertigo	9781563897153	APR078094	PREACHER VOL. 9: ALAMO	ENNIS, GARTH	DILLON, STEVE	$17.99/TP
Vertigo	9781401203153	FEB118119	PRIDE OF BAGHDAD	VAUGHAN, BRIAN K.	HENRICHON, NIKO	$14.99/TP
Vertigo	9781401220686	JUN120270	PRINCE OF CATS	WIMBERLY, RON	WIMBERLY, RON	$16.99/TP
Vertigo	9781401204006	JUL060250	THE QUITTER	PEKAR, HARVEY	HASPIEL, DEAN	$12.99/TP
Vertigo	9781401211585	SEP100300	RAT CATCHER	DIGGLE, ANDY	IBANEZ, VICTOR	$19.99/TP
Vertigo	9781401231910	JUL110280	ROAD TO PERDITION	COLLINS, MAX ALLAN	RAYNER, RICHARD PIERS	$14.99/TP
Vertigo	9781401231903	JUL110281	ROAD TO PERDITION 2: ON THE ROAD	COLLINS, MAX ALLAN	GARCIA-LOPEZ, JOSE LUIS	$14.99/TP
Vertigo	9781401223847	AUG120296	RETURN TO PERDITION	COLLINS, MAX ALLAN	BEATTY, TERRY	$14.99/TP
Vertigo	9781401222420	APR110261	REVOLVER	KINDT, MATT	KINDT, MATT	$18.99/TP
Vertigo	9781401229436	APR120279	RIGHT STATE	JOHNSON, MAT	MUTTI, ANDREA	$24.99/TP
Vertigo	9781401220839	JAN120343	SAGA OF THE SWAMP THING BOOK ONE	MOORE, ALAN	VARIOUS	$19.99/TP
Vertigo	9781401225445	JUN120283	SAGA OF THE SWAMP THING BOOK TWO	MOORE, ALAN	VARIOUS	$19.99/TP
Vertigo	9781401227678		SAGA OF THE SWAMP THING BOOK THREE	MOORE, ALAN	VARIOUS	$19.99/TP
Vertigo	9781401225759	JUL100259	THE SANDMAN VOL. 1: PRELUDES & NOCTURNES	GAIMAN, NEIL	KIETH, SAM	$19.99/TP
Vertigo	9781401227999	JUL100260	THE SANDMAN VOL. 2: THE DOLL'S HOUSE	GAIMAN, NEIL	DRINGENBERG, MIKE	$19.99/TP
Vertigo	9781401228351	JUL100261	THE SANDMAN VOL. 3: DREAM COUNTRY	GAIMAN, NEIL	JONES, KELLEY	$19.99/TP
Vertigo	9781401230425	OCT100330	THE SANDMAN VOL. 4: SEASON OF MISTS	GAIMAN, NEIL	JONES, KELLEY	$19.99/TP
Vertigo	9781401230432	JAN110431	THE SANDMAN VOL. 5: A GAME OF YOU	GAIMAN, NEIL	MCMANUS, SHAWN	$19.99/TP
Vertigo	9781401231231	MAY110287	THE SANDMAN VOL. 6: FABLES & REFLECTIONS	GAIMAN, NEIL	TALBOT, BRYAN	$19.99/TP
Vertigo	9781401232634	SEP110177	THE SANDMAN VOL. 7: BRIEF LIVES	GAIMAN, NEIL	THOMPSON, JILL	$19.99/TP
Vertigo	9781401234027	NOV110233	THE SANDMAN VOL. 8: WORLDS' END	GAIMAN, NEIL	ALLRED, MIKE	$19.99/TP
Vertigo	9781401235451	FEB120298	THE SANDMAN VOL. 9: THE KINDLY ONES	GAIMAN, NEIL	HEMPEL, MARC	$19.99/TP
Vertigo	9781401237547	AUG120292	THE SANDMAN VOL. 10: THE WAKE	GAIMAN, NEIL	ZULLI, MICHAEL	$19.99/TP
Vertigo	9781563896293	DEC068030	THE SANDMAN: THE DREAM HUNTERS	GAIMAN, NEIL	AMANO, YOSHITAKA	$19.99/TP
Vertigo	9781401224288	JUN100280	THE SANDMAN: THE DREAM HUNTERS	GAIMAN, NEIL	RUSSELL, P. CRAIG	$19.99/TP
Vertigo	9781401201135	DEC068187	THE SANDMAN: ENDLESS NIGHTS	GAIMAN, NEIL	RUSSELL, P. CRAIG	$19.99/TP
Vertigo	9781563893872	STAR07811	THE SANDMAN: THE COLLECTED DUSTCOVERS	MCKEAN, DAVE	MCKEAN, DAVE	$24.95/TP
Vertigo	9781401233327	AUG110277	THE ANNOTATED SANDMAN VOL. 1	GAIMAN, NEIL	VARIOUS	$49.99/HC
Vertigo	9781401235666	JUN120271	THE ANNOTATED SANDMAN VOL. 2	GAIMAN, NEIL	VARIOUS	$49.99/HC
Vertigo	9781401204876	JUN050447	THE SANDMAN PRESENTS: THESSALY - WITCH FOR HIRE	WILLINGHAM, BILL	MCMANUS, SHAWN	$12.99/TP
Vertigo	9781401210553	MAY080258	THE SANDMAN PRESENTS: DEAD BOY DETECTIVES	BRUBAKER, ED	TALBOT, BRYAN	$12.99/TP
Vertigo	9781401235499	AUG120295	SAUCER COUNTRY VOL. 1: RUN	CORNELL, PAUL	KELLY, RYAN	$14.99/TP
Vertigo	9781401213176	APR108251	SCALPED VOL. 1: INDIAN COUNTRY	AARON, JASON	GUERA, R.M.	$14.99/TP
Vertigo	9781401216542	NOV070301	SCALPED VOL. 2: CASINO BOOGIE	AARON, JASON	GUERA, R.M.	$14.99/TP
Vertigo	9781401218182	JUN080304	SCALPED VOL. 3: DEAD MOTHERS	AARON, JASON	GUERA, R.M.	$17.99/TP

VERTIGO SELECTED BACKLIST

IMPRINT	ISBN	DIAMOND CODE	TITLE	AUTHOR	ARTIST	US$/ FORMAT
Vertigo	9781401221799	JAN090288	SCALPED VOL. 4: THE GRAVEL IN YOUR GUTS	AARON, JASON	GUERA, R.M.	$14.99/TP
Vertigo	9781401224875	JUL090293	SCALPED VOL. 5: HIGH LONESOME	AARON, JASON	GUERA, R.M.	$14.99/TP
Vertigo	9781401227173	FEB100266	SCALPED VOL. 6: THE GNAWING	AARON, JASON	GUERA, R.M.	$14.99/TP
Vertigo	9781401230197	NOV100278	SCALPED VOL. 7: REZ BLUES	AARON, JASON	GUERA, R.M.	$17.99/TP
Vertigo	9781401232887	AUG110288	SCALPED VOL. 8: YOU GOTTA SIN TO GET SAVED	AARON, JASON	GUERA, R.M.	$17.99/TP
Vertigo	9781401235055	APR120283	SCALPED VOL. 9: KNUCKLE UP	AARON, JASON	GUERA, R.M.	$14.99/TP
Vertigo	9781401237349	JUL120253	SCALPED VOL. 10: TRAIL'S END	AARON, JASON	GUERA, R.M.	$14.99/TP
Vertigo	9781401200466	AUG080239	SHADE, THE CHANGING MAN VOL. 1: AMERICAN SCREAM	MILLIGAN, PETER	BACHALO, CHRIS	$17.99/TP
Vertigo	9781401225391	AUG080240	SHADE, THE CHANGING MAN VOL. 2: EDGE OF VISION	MILLIGAN, PETER	BACHALO, CHRIS	$19.99/TP
Vertigo	9781401227685	MAR100311	SHADE, THE CHANGING MAN VOL. 3: SCREAM TIME	MILLIGAN, PETER	HEWLETT, JAMIE	$19.99/TP
Vertigo	9781401222154	DEC110314	SHOOTERS	TRAUTMANN, ERIC AND JERWA, BRANDON	LIEBER, STEVEN	$24.99/HC
Vertigo	9781401210496	SEP080229	SILVERFISH	LAPHAM, DAVID	LAPHAM, DAVID	$17.99/TP
Vertigo	9781401203689	AUG080238	SLOTH	HERNANDEZ, GILBERT	HERNANDEZ, GILBERT	$14.99/TP
Vertigo	9781401235529	JUL120256	SPACEMAN DELUXE EDITION	AZZARELLO, BRIAN	RISSO, EDUARDO	$24.99/HC
Vertigo	9781563894701	FEB058028	STARDUST	GAIMAN, NEIL	VESS, CHARLIE	$19.99/TP
Vertigo	9781401227036	MAR110390	STUCK RUBBER BABY	CRUSE, HOWARD	CRUSE, HOWARD	$17.99/TP
Vertigo	9781401226961	AUG108007	SWEET TOOTH VOL. 1: OUT OF THE DEEP WOODS	LEMIRE, JEFF	LEMIRE, JEFF	$12.99/TP
Vertigo	9781401228545	OCT118098	SWEET TOOTH VOL. 2: IN CAPTIVITY	LEMIRE, JEFF	LEMIRE, JEFF	$12.99/TP
Vertigo	9781401231705	MAR110392	SWEET TOOTH VOL. 3: ANIMAL ARMIES	LEMIRE, JEFF	LEMIRE, JEFF	$14.99/TP
Vertigo	9781401233617	OCT110206	SWEET TOOTH VOL. 4: ENDANGERED SPECIES	LEMIRE, JEFF	LEMIRE, JEFF	$16.99/TP
Vertigo	9781401237233	JUL120259	SWEET TOOTH VOL. 5: UNNATURAL HABIT	LEMIRE, JEFF	LEMIRE, JEFF	$14.99/TP
Vertigo	9781401220846	DEC080220	TRANSMETROPOLITAN VOL. 1: BACK ON THE STREET	ELLIS, WARREN	ROBERTSON, DARICK	$14.99/TP
Vertigo	9781401222611	FEB090264	TRANSMETROPOLITAN VOL. 2: LUST FOR LIFE	ELLIS, WARREN	ROBERTSON, DARICK	$14.99/TP
Vertigo	9781401223120	DEC088262	TRANSMETROPOLITAN VOL. 3: YEAR OF THE BASTARD	ELLIS, WARREN	ROBERTSON, DARICK	$14.99/TP
Vertigo	9781401224905	JUL090291	TRANSMETROPOLITAN VOL. 4: THE NEW SCUM	ELLIS, WARREN	ROBERTSON, DARICK	$14.99/TP
Vertigo	9781401228194	SEP090228	TRANSMETROPOLITAN VOL. 5: LONELY CITY	ELLIS, WARREN	ROBERTSON, DARICK	$14.99/TP
Vertigo	9781401228187	DEC090284	TRANSMETROPOLITAN VOL. 6: GOUGE AWAY	ELLIS, WARREN	ROBERTSON, DARICK	$14.99/TP
Vertigo	9781401228156	FEB110264	TRANSMETROPOLITAN VOL. 7: SPIDER'S THRASH	ELLIS, WARREN	ROBERTSON, DARICK	$14.99/TP
Vertigo	9781401228368	JUN100282	TRANSMETROPOLITAN VOL. 8: DIRGE	ELLIS, WARREN	ROBERTSON, DARICK	$14.99/TP
Vertigo	9781401230494	JAN110435	TRANSMETROPOLITAN VOL. 9: THE CURE	ELLIS, WARREN	ROBERTSON, DARICK	$14.99/TP
Vertigo	9781401231248	MAY110296	TRANSMETROPOLITAN VOL. 10: ONE MORE TIME	ELLIS, WARREN	ROBERTSON, DARICK	$19.99/TP
Vertigo	9781401223489	FEB090267	UNCLE SAM DELUXE EDITION	DARNALL, STEVE	ROSS, ALEX	$19.99/HC
Vertigo	9781401223113	MAY090251	UNKNOWN SOLDIER VOL. 1: HAUNTED HOUSE	DYSART, JOSHUA	PONTICELLI, ALBERTO	$9.99/TP
Vertigo	9781401226008	DEC090283	UNKNOWN SOLDIER VOL. 2: EASY KILL	DYSART, JOSHUA	PONTICELLI, ALBERTO	$17.99/TP
Vertigo	9781401228552	AUG100276	UNKNOWN SOLDIER VOL. 3: DRY SEASON	DYSART, JOSHUA	PONTICELLI, ALBERTO	$14.99/TP
Vertigo	9781401231767	FEB110268	UNKNOWN SOLDIER VOL. 4: BEAUTIFUL WORLD	DYSART, JOSHUA	PONTICELLI, ALBERTO	$14.99/TP